Improving Student Test Scores

by Herman Blau

Test Scores

Winning the Game without Losing Your Soul

by Herman Blau

2nd Printing

For Information on Workshops, Visit
www.questeducationsystems.com

Improving Student Test Scores

Winning the Game without Losing Your Soul

GreenLeaf Education, LLC
320 Ichord Avenue
STE H #208
Waynesville, MO 65583
www.greenleafnow.com

Edition ISBNs

Softcover	978-1-936302-00-0
PDF	978-1-936302-01-7

Lead Editor	Mike Prater, EdD
Editor	Judith Learmann
Cover Design	Bryan Snider
	www.bryansnider.com

Contents

A Note from the Author

I have based this book on my series of *Improving Test Scores* workshops that have become popular around the nation. Presenters from my company Quest Education Systems have given tools to thousands of teachers around the nation to help students increase their knowledge, test-taking skills, and confidence. Using these tools have resulted in very real increases in student performance. It thrills me to know that I can share these same concepts with you in this book format.

I've been gratified by the supreme professionalism and dedication that I see from teachers when personally meeting countless educators in states all over this country. I see in their eyes a passion for teaching and a true love for kids. I hear from them a desire to make a difference in the lives of others. As a father of six children myself, I'm pleased to know that our nation's young people are in good hands when they go to school.

At the same time, I'm astounded by the intensity of feelings when teachers discuss the topic of standardized test scores. Teachers everywhere are feeling the pressure that comes from school accountability. They really want their kids to perform well. In fact, they take it personally when they don't! But they are feeling apprehensive, stressed, a bit confused, and sometimes even fearful. In effect, teachers are feeling that they are *losing their souls* in pursuit of higher test scores.

I want to help. With input from teachers and administrators, my team and I have developed concrete strategies that work in classrooms everywhere. These are tools that you can use to raise test scores in your school and make a difference in kids' lives. My supreme hope is that your children will increase their knowledge, motivation, and confidence to meet challenges beyond a test at the end of the year.

Relax. Take a deep breath. You are the professional. You know what is best for your students. You *can* see test scores improve, and you don't have to lose your teacher's soul in the process.

Herman Blau

About the Author

Herman Blau is a dynamic educator who has spent ten years working with teachers and administrators across the nation. An award-winning teacher, administrator, college professor and national presenter, Herman has learned how to make a difference in the lives of students and teachers.

As an expert in standardized testing and data analysis, Herman brings a wealth of knowledge on the inner working of the scoring process to help educators apply strategies for maximizing student performance on tests.

Acknowledgements

I want to thank numerous people for their help on this book:

My wife Melissa for all her love and encouragement.

My business partner and good friend Mark Eagleburger.

Casey Blau and Tom Kitchen, who have been instrumental in developing the concepts for this book.

My friend Dr. Mike Prater, the editor of Greenleaf Education.

Mrs. Judy Learmann for her invaluable editing expertise.

INTRODUCTION TO HIGH-STAKES TESTING

Some of the Boring Stuff

You Might Want to Skip this Section

Accountability in U.S. Education

Every adult connected to a public school is aware of the accountability associated with educating young people. In fact, most students know that test scores are really, really important—at least to their teachers! Oh, those scores. Why *are* they so significant to what we do in schools?

Today's basic school reform policy in the United States revolves around strong accountability requirements based primarily on student scores from a single high-stakes test. Many states have historically tried to measure student achievement by various means with different degrees of responsibility placed on schools. The landmark *No Child Left Behind Act of 2001* (NCLB) directly involved the federal government for the first time in broad-based school accountability.

NCLB substantially increased the testing requirements for states and set demanding standards for schools, districts, and states. The extensive law established adequate yearly progress (AYP) objectives for students and subgroups of students defined by socio-economic background, race, disability, and English language proficiency.

The NCLB Act has been implemented in stages, with all public school students in the nation now tested in language arts and mathematics in grades 3 through 8 and once in each of the two subject areas in high school.

Content standards, the rigor of the tests, and the definition of proficiency levels have been left to individual states, resulting in wide application of the federal mandates. Consequently, the percentage of students who score at the proficient level or higher on the state assessments varies widely from state to state. Some states have farther to go than others to meet the mandated target of 100% of students scoring proficient in language arts and mathematics by 2014 (Linn, et al. 2002).

Consequences imposed by the NCLB Act on schools, districts, and states not meeting benchmark targets have resulted in policy changes across the nation. Like never before, school administrators are examining testing data and aligning resources to focus on student achievement.

Effectiveness of Testing

Broad disagreement exists regarding the effectiveness of school accountability efforts. All states have seen increases in student achievement as measured by their assessments. All subgroups have also seen growth, although efforts to narrow the achievement gaps have been disappointing.

Analysis of student achievement growth as measured by the National Assessment of Educational Progress (NAEP) shows some positive impact since its introduction. However, this single assessment did not lead to any apparent narrowing in the black-white achievement gap, although it did narrow the Hispanic-white gap (Hanushek & Raymond, 2005).

Even as legislative mandates continue to evolve, a high degree of accountability for student performance will clearly remain in place for schools in the foreseeable future. This book presents tangible strategies to help teachers and administrators meet these accountability standards.

Please keep in mind the concepts discussed in this book are very broad in nature and are based on generally accepted testing practices. However, since specific policies and procedures can vary widely from state to state, I strongly encourage you to consult your school/district testing coordinator and state department of education as you continue to work to improve student test scores.

If you had to identify, in one word, the reason why the human race has not achieved, and never will achieve, its full potential, that word would be "meetings."
– Dave Barry

Chapter 1

WELCOME TO YOUR WORLD

Doing Your Part

Using a Lens

Never Lose Your Soul

Why This Book

If you skipped the boring introduction, here's what you missed:

1. Although state and federal mandates continue to change, your school will be held to increasingly high accountability standards in the foreseeable future,
2. Accountability for the most part is measured by how well your students perform on *one* single high-stakes test, and
3. The conversation continues regarding how approiate performance on one test measures school effectiveness.

The purpose of this book is certainly not to enter the debate over the pros and cons of high-stakes tests as a measure of student and school accountability. Those of us in the trenches in classrooms every day probably don't have a real impact on those arguments, anyway.

You most likely have this book because you are being asked to increase test scores in your classroom, your school, or your district. In reality, you work with increasing numbers of students who have limitations from disabilities, socio-economic conditions, language barriers, and home inadequacies.

Even facing these challenges, you feel the very real pressure to somehow pour knowledge into their heads, motivate those who seem unmotivated, threaten them, cajole them, bribe them, and encourage the discouraged. As their mother/father figure or big sister/brother, you must discipline them, love them, and perform what seems to be an impossible task: increasing scores on a single test that is high-stakes for you but not for the students.

If kids come to us from strong, healthy families, it makes our job easier. If they do not come to us from strong, healthy families, it makes our job more important.
– Barbara Colorose

Doing Your Part

I must tell you that improving test scores is not an impossible task. This book presents some practical strategies that will enable you to give your students tools to help build their confidence, motivation, test-taking skills, and knowledge as they take *the test*.

We must first realize that we make positive changes by each of us doing our part. I think of a story a man once told about a problem that occurred at an elementary school. Maybe it's a hypothetical problem, but it might have happened. Or at least it could happen.

A piano sitting on the stage in the multi-purpose room needed to be moved. The principal called for the three strongest men in the building to move it. Maybe they were the *only* men in the building, but in any case three men came, grabbed three corners of the piano, and heaved with no success. Trying their hardest, they could budge the piano no more than a few inches.

The principal put out an all-call for everyone in the building to come to the multi-purpose room. When every person in the building stood side by side and lifted, they were able to move the piano wherever they needed. Our motto should be:

When we have something difficult to do, we stand close together and lift wherever we stand.

Increasing student performance on the test may appear at times to be as daunting as lifting the piano, but remember the motto. Possibly the students in your school performed very well on the test except the special education students or the students on free or reduced lunches. What do you do? Do you point fingers, or do you stand together? If you are a physical education teacher, your school needs you. Your school needs you if you are a second-grade teacher. Stand close together and lift where you are. Do your part.

All of you work in different contexts. Some of you teach in a classroom with 26 third graders, while some work with eight special-needs students in a self-contained setting. Some of you are administrators, literacy coaches, and art teachers. Yet each of you has a passion to help students learn and a desire to see them score well on the high-stakes test. Whatever your context or the task assigned, you can do your part to help students succeed.

Not all the ideas presented in this book will apply to you. Some will work for you and your students and some won't. That's all right. Take the ideas that work. Use them, share them, and pass them along to others. If an idea doesn't apply, leave it, and move on to one that will.

Using a Lens

In much the same way that we educators come from different backgrounds to work with young people in different contexts, students come to us with a myriad of circumstances and personalities. In the classroom I enjoyed playing the "that's me" game with kids. I would say something, and kids would raise their hands if it applied to them.

"That's me" is a great ice breaker, and it can be used on the first day of school, before a major test, or anytime when your students are nervous or apprehensive. For example, I could say, "I went out of town this summer," and kids hold up their hands, "that's me." I might say, "I have a younger brother or sister," or "I was born in another state."

Not only does the little game help break tension and enable students to express themselves, but if used in the right way, it can give you as a teacher valuable insight into the children in your class.

The key to properly differentiating our resources for students is to be able first to know them, understand them, and look at the world through their eyes.

Many of us wear glasses, contact lenses, or we have lasik surgery so that we can see more clearly. In this book I want to give you a lens so that you can see your students more clearly and help them improve individually.

Too many times we look at students as a group and make instructional decisions based on certain outcomes without taking into consideration the individual needs and personalities of students. For example, a school might make a decision to place all students who score 2 on the test in mandatory after-school tutoring.

A policy of this sort has good intentions, but the question arises as to what we will do with the children in the sessions. Will we drill them on the basics or give them worksheets that look like the test and hope that somehow their knowledge increases enough to raise their scores? What if a student has the knowledge but is totally un-motivated? Placing him in mandatory tutoring will most likely not encourage him to work harder.

> *There is a brilliant child locked*
> *inside every student.*
> *– Marva Collins*

We raise overall test scores one student at a time by helping individual students increase their performance. The key is to see that potential inside every student and find exactly what he or she needs to improve. To have some concrete examples, I will be referring to different hypothetical children throughout this book. See if you recognize any of these students in your classes.

Amber is the intelligent, super-social eighth grader. When the phone rings at her house, nobody bothers to pick it up—it's for Amber. She is in the gifted program, band, soccer, and any other activity she can find. Amber's name is at the top of the lesson plans you leave for the substitute teacher: "Ask Amber if you have any questions." Amber always scores in the top two levels on the test, although she is very concerned that sometimes she scores a 4 instead of a 5.

Steven's name will never be on the top of the substitute's plans, at least not to ask him how to run the class. He is everything that an unmedicated fourth grade boy should be. When his dad asks him why he was kicked out of Sunday School class, he has no idea. Steven may be in the gifted program, or perhaps he could be, but he has never scored above level 2 on the test. When Steven receives the test booklet, his goal isn't to do well—his goal is to finish *first*!

Kameron is a fifth grader and has been in Title programs since preschool. Although tested several times, he never qualifies for special education services. Kameron lives with his grandmother most of the time, but his mother sometimes attends parent meetings at the school. He receives free lunches and really hasn't been much of a discipline problem at school. Kameron appears not to be motivated for the standardized test. No matter how much tutoring or special help the school gives him, Kameron has always scored in the lowest two levels on the test.

Alana doesn't stand out in her sixth-grade class. She is quite intelligent but certainly not social or popular in school. She never receives a phone call at home. When her mother asks what she did at recess, she always replies, "I read." Alana turns in her homework on time, makes high grades, and is never a discipline problem. Her level of stress increases as the test approaches.

Although she desperately wants to score well, Alana has seldom scored in the proficient category.

Melissa is in the seventh grade now and has been in the English Language Learner (ELL) program since her family moved into the district midway through last year. Her family is part of a larger group from an Eastern European country who has settled in the community over the past few years. Melissa is bright and wants to please her teachers, but her language skills are a barrier to her performance. English is rarely spoken in her home. Although Melissa does fairly well on the math portion of the test, she struggles on the language arts subtest.

Troy is a third grader who makes average grades but is a slow reader. He is very deliberate in all his work and turns in his assignments on time, but his mother comments about how long it takes him to finish his homework now that he is in the third grade. The school strongly considered retaining Troy in both kindergarten and first grade. He is bright, exhibits uncommon problem-solving skills, and scores very well on math algorithms, but Troy's slow reading skills inhibit his performance on the standardized test.

I will give you a lens in this book to begin looking individually at students such as these six and discern the best tools you can use to help them improve their performance. In the process, you will see increased motivation and confidence and higher overall achievement.

Let's put our heads together and see what life
we will make for our children.
– Chief Sitting Bull

Achievement vs. Performance

For purposes of discussion in this book, I define performance as students' scores on a single test—the mandated, annual high-stakes test. On the other hand, achievement is seen as an accumulation of student performance on a variety of assessments given over a period of time.

Think about Dustin Hoffman, a favorite actor of mine. Dustin has a long and successful career spanning over 40 years. He has starred in over 50 films and plays, twice winning the Oscar for Best Actor for his performances in *Rainman* and *Kramer vs. Kramer*. But he also starred in *Ishtar* in 1987. The movie bombed at the box office and was featured in *The Fifty Worst Movies Ever Made*.

You would be sorely misled if you happened to pick *Ishtar* as the single measurement of Dustin Hoffman's career. Taking that performance, you might score Dustin Hoffman as a very mediocre actor, but scoring his performances over the length of his career, you find an achievement which few actors have accomplished.

Most of us understand that student achievement is effectively measured over time using a variety of evaluations. But accountability in the education world today is measured by how students perform on one single assessment. We may not like it; we may feel it's unfair; and we may not think it accurately portrays what we do as educators, but it is the game that we must play. We have to teach our students to play that game to the best of their ability.

I like to ask, "What do we do when kids don't know how to read?" We teach them to read. "What do we do when kids can't do math?" We teach them to do math. But what do we do when they don't know how to take a test? Many times we try to teach them more math or reading when we should be teaching them how to take a test.

In many ways we are teaching our students to play school for the purposes of scoring well on the test. We can never forget that our students are learning to perform in a variety of life settings and on numerous informal assessments given in and out of school. It would be silly for us to think that the test we give them once a year is the only performance score that is important to them, or that it is important to them at all. They are working every day to become proficient in their real world—their environment.

Most of us educators come from a middle- or upper-middle class background. School was fairly easy for us, and we liked it for the most part. We were effective in school and performed well on most assessments the school gave us.

Now imagine you were placed as a young person (or even now for that matter) in an inner-city gang situation. You might very well be killed because you don't have the knowledge or the language needed to survive. You would need to quickly learn the application skills to manage in an environment that is foreign to you.

Playing School

Many of the students in your classroom are trying to survive in an environment that is foreign to them. A large part of our jobs as educators is to teach some of our children to play school in order to perform in our world.

Let me give you an example. Suppose you give students half-credit for work turned in late. A perfect paper turned in late will be worth 50% in the gradebook. Many at-risk students don't see the value in turning the paper in late, because it's still an F, isn't it?

On the other hand, the student who understands the process knows that 50% averaged with his other grades makes a difference versus the 0% that he currently has. That student probably has parents who push him to get the work turned in because they know the value of at least half-credit points. But many students don't have the support system at home to teach them the rules of school. An increasingly essential task for teachers is to help students at risk of failure learn how to play school in an environment that may be foreign to them.

Improving Test Scores

Remember the title of this book is *Improving Student Test Scores*. I make no apology that I am focusing on the skills that you can use to help your students improve scores on a single test.

I understand the natural resistance we have to that notion, because, after all, we teach math, reading, writing, science, and all the other important things. Do we really want to teach test-taking skills to kids? Yes, we do.

The ability to score well on a single test is rapidly becoming a life skill. Think of the many applications where a person must take a test: to enter college, to join the military, to become a policeman, a firefighter, an EMT, a hairdresser, or even a teacher. The list is almost endless.

Giving our students skills to prepare adequately, reduce text anxiety, organize answers, and pace themselves when testing will be invaluable to them in life.

I also understand the normal opposition to the notion of teaching to the test. But if the standards are appropriate and the test assesses those standards, isn't it fitting for us to expect students to perform well on those objectives?

When I ask teachers some of the reasons students do poorly on the test, I hear many thoughts: they can't read, they have a poor home life, they have no motivation, and so on. But never does a teacher say that it's because the test isn't appropriate. It may be too difficult for some students, but the issue isn't with the test. For the most part we must agree that the objectives covered by the test are skills that students should know.

Winning the Game without Losing Your Soul

On the other hand, the subtitle of the book reads *How to Win the Game without Losing Your Soul.* We are professional educators, and we know what our students need to master before they leave us and transition to the next level. We have pacing guides, curriculum guides, assessments, and a host of support materials to direct us.

The test is just that: only one test. It is a high-stakes test, but it is just one assessment. We cannot give in to the idea that we must focus all our efforts during the year on preparing students for the one test.

Don't allow your own anxiety about test results to drive what you must do as a professional educator. You don't have to lose your individuality or your connection with your students. You can adequately prepare them for the test and still retain your creativity to be an effective and caring teacher.

Relax. You *can* see scores improve without losing your soul. This book will show you how to analyze individual student needs and give them necessary skills for the test. You will learn how to determine the objectives that are most important for you, the ones on which to focus your limited resources. Techniques found in this book will help you write effective assessments and pace them properly throughout the year to effectively prepare your students.

Your students will have more confidence and motivation to do well on the test when they are armed with test-taking strategies. You *will* see test scores improve, one student at a time.

Cherishing children is the mark of a civilized society.
— Joan Ganz Cooney

Providence protects children and idiots. I know because I have tested it.
— Mark Twain

Chapter 2

USING THE KAM = P LENS

Getting the Most Value
for Your Effort

Defining the KAM = P

The **KAM = P score** is an instrument I've developed to more accurately assess the needs of individual students. KAM = P scores can be used to help increase performance in a variety of applications besides standardized test scores, from getting a child to do chores to improving student behavior. The applications are numerous, and I will be referring to the KAM = P tool several times in this book.

KAM = P
Knowledge x Application x Motivation = Performance

First, some definitions. *Knowledge* is the ability to read, explain the difference between a solar and lunar eclipse, know the multiplication tables, etc. A rule I like to use is this: if the student is going to use it after the test, then it's knowledge. When he is 20, will he still be reading? Yes. When she is 20, will she be using fractions and percents? Yes. Then that is knowledge.

Application refers to test-specific strategies that will help students do better on the test but aren't necessarily life-long skills. For example, having the student underline where she found the answer may help her do better on the test. Will she need to be able to do that when she is 20? Probably not, so that strategy is an application.

Motivation is just what it appears to be: the desire on the part of students to do the very best on anything they attempt. In this case, we are talking about the motivation to do their best on a test. As I talk to thousands of teachers across the nation, I hear what all of us already know intuitively. Student motivation is a huge dynamic in determining performance on tests.

By using the KAM = P lens, we can learn more about the knowledge, application, and motivation components that affect test scores. The KAM = P formula follows the rules of multiplication. Imagine that we assign a value of 0 to 9 to a student's level of knowledge, application, and motivation, with 0 representing the lowest level and 9 representing the highest.

Multiplying the three numbers together yields a single KAM = P score. As an example, think back to the six hypothetical students described in Chapter 1. Their teacher assigned them a score on the three factors and the resulting performance score:

Student	K	x	A	x	M	=	P
Amber	7		5		7	=	245
Steven	7		5		0	=	0
Kameron	1		1		1	=	1
Alana	5		1		5	=	25
Melissa	1		1		9	=	9
Troy	3		3		3	=	27

Don't we all wish we had a room full of Ambers? She will score proficient on the test regardless of who is standing in front of the room. She is bright, has wonderfully supportive parents, and wants to please her teachers. Amber may be pulled out of the class periodically for the gifted and talented program, and we somehow feel that is meeting her needs for enrichment and challenge. In fact, we don't spend a lot of time thinking about Amber because she is in the bag when it comes test time.

But think carefully about Amber, and look again at her KAM = P score. Why is her motivation score only 7? Amber does her best, and it's enough for her to score proficient, but the test isn't really important for Amber because it holds no accountability for *her*. When she takes a test that is high-stakes for *her*, like a college entrance exam, her motivation will be high. At that time, she will need some test-taking skills. Notice her application score is only 5. No one has taught Amber how to take a standardized test. Although her overall score is good enough for now, we would do her a great service by teaching her some application skills, helping lower some of her anxiety and increase her confidence for a test.

Steven is frustrating to teachers, scoring zero on motivation. He has the knowledge and some application skills, but he never performs on the test to the level that we expect. An assortment of reasons explain why Steven doesn't perform: he just doesn't see why doing well on the test affects him; he is a speedster and wants to be the first one finished; or it may even be a deliberate form of rebellion for him to do poorly.

What usually happens if we place Steven in a tutoring program to work on knowledge? He acts out, doesn't he? He begrudges the system that placed him somewhere he knows he doesn't belong. He becomes a waste of your time and a distraction to others. You might be able to increase his knowledge just a bit and maybe his application a little, but his motivation may actually go down.

Now look at Kameron who scores 1 in each category. All of us have several Kamerons and a few Ambers in the same class. Kameron is low in knowledge, low in application, and low in motivation, resulting in low performance. Which of the three areas would you want to focus your energy on? Many times we work extremely hard to increase Kameron's knowledge. We put him in after-school tutoring, Title programs, remedial programs, etc. All those efforts are fine, and if administered correctly, they will most likely raise Kameron's knowledge a bit. We might raise his knowledge from a 1 to a 2 or maybe even a 3, resulting in a performance score of 3.

But what if we also taught Kameron some test-taking strategies to increase his skill? And maybe we used some motivation tactics to raise his level of involvement in the test. What would happen if we raised his knowledge only to a 2, but we also raised both his application skills and motivation to a 2? His resulting performance level would be 2 x 2 x 2, equaling a score of 8, more than twice the performance we see by working so hard to increase his knowledge to a 3 at the expense of the other two factors.

Alana has average knowledge and a good deal of motivation. We all want Alana in our class. She is a pleaser, works hard, is never a behavior problem, and turns in all her work on time. Alana's test scores just aren't what we would hope for or expect from such a good student. In fact, we never know if she will score proficient on the test. She is one of those students who are on the bubble.

Interestingly enough, if you give Alana the work at home, she will get it right every time. But when it's on a high-stakes test, she opens the booklet and shuts down. She has an extreme amount of test anxiety, she doesn't know how to begin the test, and she has no skills to help her reach a performance level that is equal to her ability. We most likely don't need to motivate Alana. She could be placed in tutoring and possibly increase her knowledge level from 5 to 6. But what if we focused on her application skills, raising her score from 1 to 5? That would raise her performance level to 125, easily enough for her to score proficient every year.

Melissa may be your English Language Learner or a student with special needs. She loves her teachers, is highly motivated, and will do anything you ask her. She really wants to do well on the test, but she simply doesn't have the knowledge. Frustrated, she approaches the upcoming test with anxiety, afraid she will fail once again.

A wide variety of helpful programs exist to help improve improve Melissa's knowledge. But what if we raised her knowledge level to merely a 2, and also gave her strategies to improve her application level to a 4 or 5? Melissa would greatly increase her performance and might even score proficient on the test.

Troy is a hard–working third grader we would also welcome in our class. He is seldom a discipline problem and turns in his homework on time; however, his motivation for the test is only 3. His grades are consistently only average, and he most likely won't score at the proficient level on the test. He has strong problem-solving skills and does very well on math algorithms, but he is a slow reader. His reading comprehension seems to be average, but his deliberate approach to his work inhibits his performance on the test.

Troy's KAM = P scores indicate his average to below-average performance. Notice his teacher has given him a 3 in all areas. Most likely we need to focus our attention in all three areas, raising Troy's scores from 3 to 5 across the board. Doing so would raise his performance score by a multiple of 5; easily enough for him to score proficient.

Every child comes with a message that God
is not yet discouraged of man.
– Rabindranath Tagore

Getting the Most Value for Your Effort

Now think about a student in your room right now who you want to see improve performance on the standardized test. Give him or her a KAM = P score. What level would he or she have on the knowledge factor? application? motivation? Write the levels down and multiply for an overall performance score.

Student	K	x	A	x	M	=	P
_____	___	x	___	x	___	=	___

What do you learn about the student? Is he low in every area? You need to spread out your efforts. Is he low in only one area? You need to focus your efforts. Do you need to pump him up in motivation? Practice test-taking strategies? Now circle the one area that gives you the most value for your effort!

No one works harder or cares more for student performance than you, the classroom teacher. Your time is the most valuable and rarest commodity you have to share with students. Use the KAM = P tool to focus your efforts to get the most use of the little time you have with each student.

The scores are obviously very subjective, but as with all scoring guides, you can develop some informal guidelines to apply that will place a level of consistency across your class. After all, no one knows your children like you do! The KAM = P instrument gives us a lens to look through as we work with students, a starting point to identify individual needs and how they have an impact on test scores. The tool might even give us a new way to look at our students overall.

Every student can learn, just not on the same day,
or in the same way.
– George Evans

Knowledge, Application, or Motivation?

For organization purposes, discussing the three factors as separate components would be beneficial. In actual practice, though, many times the lines between the three are blurry, especially the line between knowledge and application. In the chapters that follow, you will easily notice some topics that fit neatly into one of the factors: for example, reducing test-taking anxiety is an application skill. Other topics, such as understanding the different types of test items, don't fall as precisely into a single category.

The three factors themselves overlap when we begin applying them to real children. For example, when you help Alana reduce her test anxiety and increase her confidence, her motivation will most likely increase. That added motivation will result in her applying herself which will also increase her knowledge. If you can establish a relationship with Kameron and boost his motivation to do well just because you ask him, you will most likely see his knowledge level raise.

We can apply the terms knowledge, application, and motivation to students who don't know it, can't show it, or don't care about it.

Don't Know It

We really have only three options to address the needs of the students who have some motivation and application strategies, but little knowledge. We can work to get them the knowledge through teaching and reteaching, we can give them a tool to make them seem smarter than they really are, or we can let them fail.

I obviously don't propose that we let them fail, and for the most part this book isn't about methods of teaching and reteaching. Later chapters will offer strategies such as the brain dump and others that help students organize the knowledge they do have. These tools give them the upper hand when dealing with facts and data.

Can't Show It

Too many times teachers are frustrated because they fixate on the knowledge component without considering other factors that contribute to test performance. We can let them fail, or we can give students tools to become better test takers. We can teach them effective strategies to boost confidence and test scores.

Remember the very real notion that teaching students how to successfully take a test is a life skill. For example, if we help them overcome test anxiety, deal with the time issue, and recognize the relationship between questions and answers, we are helping them develop competencies they can use the rest of their lives.

Don't Care about It

I have talked to thousands of teachers across the nation regarding the factors contributing to low performance on standardized tests. After they place a few of their own students into the KAM = P formula, I ask which of the factors they believe contribute the most to low scores. A few indicate that knowledge is the issue, a few more point toward application strategies, but the vast majority say that motivation is the leading cause of poor performance.

Nothing is wrong with realizing some students need more knowledge. Hey, we all could use more knowledge! But how are students typically tutored in preparation for the test? We keep them after school and put them in the back of the room around the kidney-shaped table. We work on increasing their knowledge, and we might address the application factor just a bit.

We seldom work on student motivation, unless we believe that keeping students after school for an hour of tutoring will raise it. Forcing students to work longer and harder doesn't act as a deterrent, nor does it bring about increased motivation. As they sit in that tutoring session, very few of them are thinking, "Boy, I want to do better on the test this year so I won't have to stay after school next year!" How many of us adults would respond to that idea of motivation?

If a child doesn't have motivation, then you as a teacher must become a master motivator.

Write down in your heart, "I am a master motivator. I am a teacher, and I motivate others to do their best."

Is the answer to increased performance simply increased student motivation? No, but neither is it improved test-taking strategies or increased knowledge. The answer lies in seeing students through a lens to determine what component they most need in order to help them succeed.

Which Is Most Important?

A discussion always arises regarding which of the three factors are most significant in determining test scores. Many people instinctively believe that motivation is the multiplier in the KAM = P formula, the most important of the three to raise performance. I have no doubt that motivation is essential to boosting performance in all areas of student outcomes. But I hesitate to make the claim that it is the most important, because then we seem to be reducing performance to bribing students to do well on a test. That is absolutely not the message I want to be sending.

Of course, motivating students is much more involved than bribing them. Motivation equated with just a prize at the end certainly isn't a multiplier in the formula.

To be the most powerful influence in a young person's life, a teacher must establish a meaningful relationship with that child. The truth is, if you can powerfully and deeply touch students' lives, the areas of knowledge and application will increase as they work their heart out for you.

The kids in our classroom are infinitely more significant than the subject matter we teach.
– Meladee McCarty

Using the Lens

Looking again at the KAM = P instrument, we realize that moving students from 1 to 9 on any factor is incredibly difficult. Honestly, moving them from 1 to 2 is easier than moving them from 8 to 9. Don't get fixated on making all your students score 9 on every factor. Your time is better used to move them up a bit in every area. Remember, you want to get the most value for your effort!

Teacher Story

A middle school teacher in Texas came up to me during the break in one of my workshops after I had discussed using the KAM = P tool. He related how he had just finished spending two weeks with his students preparing for the test. They worked in class; they worked after school. He worked like never before. He had just received the test results, and they were extremely disappointing. The scores showed some slight improvement, but nothing like he was expecting after all that work.

"I'm not doing that again," he said. "It was too much work. But you know, I just realized that I never once talked about application strategies. And I didn't give a thought to motivating them except making them work hard on increasing their knowledge."

Most teachers can relate to the previous story. We work hard, do everything we can to help increase performance, and in frustration, we figuratively throw up our hands and say to the students, "Why aren't you doing better?" And the answer is because we haven't used a lens to look at individual students as related to their test scores.

We think too much about effective methods of teaching and not enough about effective methods of learning.
– John Carolus S.J.

Other KAM = P Applications

Many teachers tell me that they give their entire class a KAM = P score as it relates to behavior. Are the students acting out because they don't have knowledge? Maybe they are misbehaving out of frustration. Or are they acting out because they don't have application skills? Possibly they need to be taught the processes to behave in a school setting.

Teachers have told me they realize they have missed out on the motivation piece by not establishing relationships with students and their parents. They are spending an inordinate amount of time on what they think is motivation, but all they are doing is giving out stars. The KAM = P process has caused them to reexamine their motivation plan.

In many schools, a teacher brings the name of a student at risk of failing to the Student Assistance Team (SAT), convened to help the teacher find interventions. The team gives the teacher suggestions: maybe sitting the student closer to the front or possibly assigning tutoring.

When the teacher comes back in six weeks and says the student is still struggling, the team either assigns testing for the student or gives the poor teacher more suggestions to try. Many times an effective method for identifying the exact problem(s) facing the student is missing.

I suggest the SAT use a four-step process incorporating the KAM = P lens:

1. *Unburden.* In this step the teacher first relates to the team all the symptoms. She talks about grades, homework, behavior, and attitude. She discusses everything thing that is wrong with the student. The teacher is allowed to express her frustration and tells the team about all the interventions she has tried for the student.

2. *Clarification.* Each member of the team asks clarifying questions: "Tell me more about . . ." The team may ask more about the student's home life, work habits, grades, behavior in special classes or on the playground, or anything that comes to mind.

3. *Identification.* The teacher of the at-risk student then uses the KAM = P tool to help identify some core problems. This gives the teacher an opportunity to reframe the student in the lens of a KAM = P score and discover some key knowledge, application, or motivation issues that might be causing the student's difficulties.

4. *Self-discovery.* Now with a more accurate diagnosis, the teacher can begin to develop some strategies that lead to a solution. At this time the other members of the team give input, and working to-

gether, they outline an effective plan to help the student succeed.

My own daughter recently went through a lengthy process of allergy testing after developing a rash. What would have happened if on the first visit, the doctor looked at the rash and told us that she had to quit drinking milk? We would have taken her off milk products because, after all, he is the expert, and lactose intolerance is a fairly common problem. But instead, the doctor began a series of tests, administering a pinprick one by one, eliminating allergy after allergy, until he found the one causing her rash.

The analogy to education is obvious. If we never diagnose correctly, we will never find the correct solution. We must use tools to properly examine students through a lens that allows us to reach the root of the problem.

I like a teacher who gives you something to take home to think about besides homework.
– Lily Tomlin as "Edith Ann"

Chapter 3

ASSESSMENT

TO GUIDE

LEARNING

Increasing Knowledge

Testing the Right Thing at the Right Time

Formative vs. Summative Assessments

Because the role of assessments in guiding student learning has received so much attention lately, many schools have made efforts to align them with learning objectives. In addition, schools have established protocols for teachers and administrators to evaluate student assessment data in order to guide instruction.

This isn't a book about the appropriate use of assessments, but I do think examining the role of summative and formative assessments, especially as they relate to the knowledge component of the KAM = P lens, is vital. You will find a list of references at the back of this book pertinent to the subject of assessments. Two resources I have found especially helpful are *Ahead of the Curve*, edited by Doug Reeves, and James Popham's *Transformative Assessment*.

Let's first define the difference between summative and formative assessments.

Summative Assessment

Summative Assessment refers to the assessment *of* learning and summarizes the performance of students at a particular moment in time.

After a period of work such as a unit, a semester, or at the end of a year, the student sits for a test that is graded and given a score. The test aims to summarize learning up to that point. In that sense, a measurement of this type is the assessment *of* the learning that has taken place.

If given in small increments, the summative tests can be used for diagnostic assessment and identify individual weaknesses that guide instructional decisions. The more summative in nature the assessments are, that is, the longer the span of instruction between testing, the more difficult it becomes to change teaching practices to improve student performance.

The high-stakes tests discussed in this book are particularly ill-suited for helping teachers improve their instruction or modify their approach to individual students. Schools typically give tests of this type near the end of the year when instructional activities are drawing to a close. The results aren't given to teachers until several months later, and by that time the students have moved on to other classrooms with different teachers.

On the other hand, formative assessments occur while content is being taught and learned and should continue throughout the period of learning.

Formative Assessment

Formative Assessment refers to assessment *for* learning. It is a process used during instruction that provides feedback to adjust ongoing teaching and learning to improve students' achievement.

The primary objective of formative assessments is not to assign grades, but rather to inform the teacher and students of what they know or do not know. More important, classroom formative assessments allow teachers to monitor their instruction and make decisions based on immediate student performance (Ainsworth, 2006). Measurements of this type are assessments *for* learning.

The Assessment Continuum

I like to use the analogy of a formative assessment being akin to a physical checkup. When I go to the doctor and get a formative assessment, I'm given a series of tests to determine my overall health. The doctor might find I'm a bit overweight and tell me, "Herman, you need to lay off the Whoppers™, eat more apples, and get more exercise." The summative assessment is when I'm on the autopsy table. They open me up and say, "Herman should have laid off the Whoppers™, eaten more apples, and exercised more." It's too late at that point to change the outcome.

We must develop a program of appropriate formative assessments during the year to ensure our students are on track to master the objectives on the summative exam. My friend Mike Prater has developed an assessment continuum found on the following page to give teachers a graphical representation of the role assessments play in driving instructional decisions.

None of us got where we are solely by pulling ourselves up by our bootstraps. We got here because somebody – a parent, a teacher, an Ivy League crony, or a few nuns – bent down and helped us pick up our boots.
– Thurgood Marshall

The Assessment Continuum
by Mike Prater, EdD
© 2008. Used with permission.

Classroom/Team Level
- Takes place during instruction
- A process, not just a test
- Used by teachers and students to make adjustments in order to improve achievement

Formative
What do we need to change?

Classroom/Team Level
- At the end of a unit of instruction
- Various types of assessments
- Based on chronological pacing
- Allows for reteaching and differentiated instruction

Intermediary
How are we doing?

District/Building Level
- Typically given once a year
- High-stakes/Accountability
- Used to measure performance of a student or a group of students at one instant in time

Summative
How have we done?

Aligning the Curriculum

We must properly align and pace our curriculum with the objectives covered on the test in order to ensure all the standards are adequately covered. That process can be difficult, given the amount of material we face and the short amount of time we have in a school year. I hear many teachers comment that they have more curriculum than calendar.

Teacher Story

Shayla is in her third year of teaching. She has 28 fifth graders in her classroom this year. Three of the students are in the special education program, and four probably should be, but didn't test into it. Two students are pulled out three times per week for the ELL program, and four are pulled out three times per week for the Title I program. Two of her students leave one day per week for the gifted/talented program. The most recent DRA test indicated that exactly one-half of her students are still reading below grade level. The math textbook has 14 chapters, but by midyear she has covered only five of them.

I'm sure you can sympathize with Shayla. You most likely teach in a heterogeneous classroom composed of students with a wide range of abilities. Now suppose the math textbook has 14 chapters. You can choose to go a mile wide and an inch thick to get through the book, or you can slow down and ensure every student masters the concepts through Chapter 9. What happens if the geometry objectives that are on the test are covered in Chapter 11, and you don't get there?

The solution is first to identify exactly what we expect every student to know. We begin by looking at national and state standards and frameworks, and then at the breakdown of objectives covered on the state assessment. To be honest, some concepts in textbooks are just not essential for students to know.

Several education leaders write about the need to stop doing stuff. Many times we pile more and more objectives into our curriculum without considering the things that we should remove. Sometimes to stop doing stuff is actually more difficult than to cover additional objectives. Remember that we want the most value for our effort, so let's spend our time on the basic standards that we know will be on the test.

> The secret is knowing exactly what standards will be on the high-stakes test, how many items will be taken from each of the standards, and what form the items will take on the test. In addition, what level of knowledge will the items address?

The teacher who finds students having success on the test is one who directs his or her efforts from the first day of the school year toward those objectives that will be on the test. That teacher doesn't exclusively cover those objectives, but in a systematic manner uses assessments to ensure that students have mastered the essential concepts.

Having a system in place from the beginning allows the teacher to reach the end of the year with a much lower stress level than otherwise. The teacher also finds that he or she has time to cover the other things during the year.

Grant Wiggins and Jay McTighe (2005) discuss the concept of "backward design" when developing curriculum and assessments. The notion is to write an instructional plan with the end in mind. That is, first determine the objectives students need to master, write the assessment that you will use to determine if they have learned the objectives, and then develop the instructional plan to teach to those objectives.

Pacing the Assessments

The same concept works well when preparing students for the annual test. Most state departments of education have done a good job of communicating the standards that they will assess on their test, the percentage of items that test each standard, and the test item depth of knowledge level. The Appendix lists websites for all fifty departments of education with instructions to link to the correct page within each department. Your building and/or district test coordinator will also have detailed information regarding the makeup of the test. Be sure you understand exactly what your students will be expected to know and how they will be assessed.

Most states also have a method to allow schools to find out how students have performed on past tests. They usually release data that let schools determine what their students scored by standard and disaggregate down to at least the building and/or classroom level. Administrators typically have the only access to these data because of privacy concerns, but make sure your school is using all the tools available to help students.

Although summative in nature, examining data from past tests allows schools to see a pattern in item analysis and to determine which standards their students are struggling with.

On pages 56-57 you will find an analysis that a hypothetical school completed for its performance over the past three years on the state's 4th grade math test.

The objectives as coded by the state appears on the left in the chart. This state codes the math standards by the National Council of Teachers of Mathematics (NCTM) standards, A stands for algebraic relationships, D means data and probability, G is geometry, M represents measurement, and N equates to numbers and operations. So, A1 represents the first objective on the algebra standard, A2 is the second objective on that standard, and so on.

You can easily substitute your state's coding for the standards/objectives/key skills that appear on the test.

Here is a portion of the table, with the objectives highlighted:

Obj.	# Items	Avg. %
A1		
D3		
G1		
M2		
N3		

The next column in the chart lists the number of items on the test from the objective:

Obj.	# Items	Avg. %
A1	3	
D3	4	
G1	6	
M2	1	
N3	1	

The final column shows the average percentage of the students in the school who answered the item correctly:

Obj.	# Items	Avg. %
A1	3	84%
D3	4	92%
G1	6	79%
M2	1	76%
N3	1	85%

Now you can add dimension to the table by taking a longitudinal look at the data over the past three years:

	3 yrs ago			2 yrs ago			Last yr	
Obj.	# Items	Avg %		# Items	Avg %		# Items	Avg %
A1	3	84%		2	71%		3	71%
D3	4	92%		7	92%		4	93%
G1	6	79%		7	77%		2	92%
M2	1	76%		2	55%		1	36%
N3	1	85%		2	82%		4	85%

Just looking at this abbreviated version of the data gives us some guidance. For example, I see that students haven't done very well on objective M2, especially in the last couple of years. But do you really want to exert great effort on an objective that may have only one or two items?

On the other hand, students have done very well on objective D3. But I would think the school wants to emphasize that objective during the year because historically quite a few items from that objective are on the test.

Two methods determine what I call the *power objectives*: either find the objectives that have been tested most often or identify the objectives that your students have been struggling with. Armed with these two ideas in mind, you can quickly identify the areas to direct your resources.

The next two pages depict the entire study of the hypothetical school.

Somewhere Elementary School
Annual Comparisons
4th Grade Mathematics Item Analysis

Obj.	3 yrs ago # Items	3 yrs ago Avg %		2 yrs ago # Items	2 yrs ago Avg %		Last yr # Items	Last yr Avg %
A1	3	84%		2	71%		3	71%
A2	2	59%		2	74%		1	50%
A3								
A4								
A5	5	78%		2	71%		3	80%
A6				1	89%		1	75%
A7	1	55%		2	47%		1	39%
A8				1	89%		1	58%
D1								
D2								
D3	4	92%		7	92%		4	93%
D4	2	74%		2	81%		4	68%
D5								
D6	2	63%		2	87%		3	50%
D7								
G1	6	79%		7	77%		2	99%
G2								
G3	2	69%					2	84%
G4	2	74%		3	71%		1	74%
G5	2	74%		1	93%		2	72%
G6	2	74%		1	93%		3	84%
G7	2	71%		1	84%		2	83%

Somewhere Elementary School
Annual Comparisons
4th Grade Mathematics Item Analysis
(continued)

Obj.	3 yrs ago			2 yrs ago			Last yr	
	# Items	Avg %		# Items	Avg %		# Items	Avg %
M1				1	74%		1	75%
M2	1	76%		2	55%		1	36%
M3	2	94%					2	72%
M4	3	66%		2	74%		1	55%
M5	3	74%		4	60%		2	62%
M6							3	74%
M7	3	64%		3	49%		3	84%
M8								
N1							1	84%
N2	2	82%		2	75%			
N3	1	85%		2	82%		4	85%
N4				1	78%			
N5	3	78%		3	65%		5	82%
N6								
N7								
N8	7	79%		7	78%		6	78%
N9	4	58%		3	69%		3	79%
N10								

Organized data analysis of this sort accompanied with a systematic plan to teach and assess the most important objectives effectively prepares students for the test. Without it, our efforts become merely a whack-a-mole type of plan each year, focusing on some objectives one year, and then some others the following year as they pop up.

A quick look at the full chart gives you some valuable information. In addition to objective D3 mentioned earlier, I notice objectives M7, N5, N8, and N9 appear frequently on the test. At the same time, I see that the school has been struggling with objectives A2, D6, M4, and M5. These nine objectives form the core of power objectives that we will focus on this year.

We can also see the objectives that aren't tested at all in fourth grade. Those objectives might show up in our curriculum guides as introduced concepts if they appear in fifth grade, but I don't feel a strong need to cover them in fourth grade.

Although states vary in standards tested, levels of performance, depths of knowledge, and types of test items, I hope you can see how you might adapt an analysis of this sort to your school.

Mapping the Assessments

The next item in our discussion is the need to assess key objectives on a formative basis. Many times we think unit tests alone are effective formative assessments. As I mentioned before, teachers can use unit tests to guide instruction, but a problem arises if we think of unit tests as the only vehicles to prepare students for the high-stakes test.

What if the objectives assessed on the standardized test aren't on unit tests? What if they are not in the same proportion or in the same format? The unit tests are merely assessing what I covered this unit. Maybe some of the test aligns with the high-stakes test, but other objectives are also on the unit test.

Also, reteaching after giving the unit test is difficult. We're moving on to the next unit and different objectives. Our remediation at that point becomes separate interventions for students who show they are struggling. A much better plan would include methods to catch struggling students early and have a more focused intervention.

The first step in the process is to identify those power objectives discussed previously. Again, power objectives are those you determine to be the most vital to student success on the test. As mentioned earlier, we can establish them in different ways: by looking at the blueprint of the test over the past three years, by finding the objectives our students have struggled with, and with our own classroom observations and assessments.

The next step is to develop a map to guide your formative assessments and pace them appropriately throughout the year. I suggest a two-pronged approach in addition to the normal assessment schedule outlined by the curriculum: daily bell-ringers and intermediary formative assessments given monthly.

Remember that you don't want to lose your soul in preparing for the high-stakes test. That means you must

1. Broadly cover all the objectives in the curriculum
2. Deeply cover the power objectives defined by your team or your school
3. Have time to meet the needs of your heterogeneous classroom

Daily bell-ringers allow the broad coverage of the objectives, while monthly formative assessments ensure deep coverage of the power objectives. A systematic plan from the beginning of the year guarantees that you won't spend an inordinate amount of time focusing on objectives. You will still have time to meet the broad needs of your students in the way that you know is best. Remember, don't lose your soul!

Daily Bell-Ringers

In a mile-wide-and-an-inch-thick approach, daily bell-ringers ensure that teachers adequately cover all test objectives during the year and at sufficient variations of Depth of Knowledge (DOK). Unless you are in a state that includes an extended performance event on the test, all items are written to three levels of DOK. The Appendix includes a sample DOK chart.

Most tests have approximately 25% of the items written to Level 1, 50% written to Level 2, and 25% written to Level 3. Many times we have concerns about students' ability to answer questions written to Level 3, but it makes sense to spend one-fourth of our time on each of Levels 1 and 3 and one-half of our time on Level 2.

A monthly chart at the top of the next page shows how you might plan your bell-ringers. The state where we find our hypothetical school tests 20 math objectives, and I've made sure all 20 appear at least once during the month. One week of the month will use items from DOK Level 1, two weeks will focus on Level 2, and one week has items from Level 3.

Monthly Chart of Bell-Ringer Objectives

Week	DOK	Mon	Tues	Wed	Thurs	Fri
1	1	A1	D3	G1	M2	N3
2	2	A2	D4	G4	M4	N5
3	2	A5	D6	G5	M5	M7
4	3	A7	G6	G7	N8	N9

I've randomly placed the objectives on the chart since I have no idea exactly what each one covers. Of course, you can adjust the objectives to your specific state and your needs, placing them as you see fit within the different levels of DOK. You might even want to place the power objectives more often on the chart if you have time. I'm sure you get the idea.

A plan of this sort ensures that you cover all objectives on the test, and it gives you some daily formative feedback coupled with your normal learning activities. This plan also allows for early classroom interventions when a student has difficulty mastering an objective.

Monthly Formative Assessments

To ensure deeper coverage of the power objectives that you have identified, I suggest monthly formative assessments that feature items very similar to those found on the standardized test. I talk frequently in this book about practicing like we play, referring to the notion that our assessments should mirror the kinds of questions on the test in quantity, type, and level of difficulty.

The chart at the top of page 63 maps by month the nine power objectives that we identified in our hypothetical school. Each month lists the number of items on our assessment from each objective, with the total items on the test listed in the column to the right.

You will notice that at the first of the year, each month has two objectives highlighted in bold that we will focus on with four questions from each. The next month has two new highlighted objectives, with the previous month's focus having only two items each. The other objectives have one item each until we have covered all of them.

This gives us a systematic manner to know that we have adequately covered all of the power objectives in the year, with review time left before the test. It also provides some additional formative data in addition to the bell-ringers and classroom activities. For example, if a student struggles in September with objectives N5 and N8, we can assign classroom interventions. If he continues to struggle with the same objectives in October, we might move him into a Tier 2 intervention. In this manner we can focus our efforts where they are most effective.

Again, I have randomly placed the objectives on the chart for purposes of illustrating how a method like this might work. You can use the format to best suit your needs.

Your heart is slightly bigger than the average human heart, but that's because you're a teacher.
– Aaron Bacall

Annual Chart of Power Objectives

	A2	D3	D6	M4	M5	M7	N5	N8	N9	Tot #
				Power Objectives						
Sep	1	1	1	1	1	1	4	4	1	15
Oct	4	1	1	4	1	1	2	2	1	17
Nov	2	4	1	2	1	1	2	2	4	19
Dec	2	2	4	2	4	1	2	2	2	21
Jan	2	2	2	2	2	4	2	2	2	20
Feb	2	2	2	2	2	2	2	2	2	18
Mar	2	2	2	2	2	2	2	2	2	18

Although many districts have paced curriculum guides, I feel strongly that we should not take complete control of the chronological pacing away from teachers. As teachers, you have the responsibility to meet the individual needs of your students. You know better than anyone else the pacing that will best prepare your students for the test. But you must have the end in mind, understanding clearly the expectations placed on students. You also need a plan in place to appropriately assess them in a formative manner throughout the year. In addition to school or district power objectives, you can determine them for your classroom based on your own data analysis.

Which objectives do you choose to put across the top of the calendar? As I've mentioned, after examining the test blueprint, I would suggest that you especially focus on the items appearing most often or those that your students struggle with. You have to decide how much time and attention you want to pay to an objective that is assessed with only one or two items on the test, even if your students are scoring 40% on that objective. Remember to get the most value for your effort.

For this outline of formative assessments to be effective, we must test the objectives that are most important. However, these assessments should not monopolize instructional time. I hear stories of districts who spend five days for formative assessments out of a 20-day instructional month. I feel spending one-quarter of instructional time assessing students is an unwise use of resources.

Teachers can use short, focused assessments such as daily bell-ringers on a formal and informal basis daily to create data informing them of the progress of individual students. Effectively analyzing these data and having collaborative discussions with other teachers allows time to catch weaknesses soon enough to implement suitable interventions. Assessments can then be *for* learning rather than *of* learning that has already taken place.

Aligning the Assessments

Allow me to go back to the assessment calendar. You will notice that I suggest you assess every power objective each month. The testing in September might be on last year's standards to establish a baseline or possibly on this year's standards as a pretest.

Exposing students to some things in September that they haven't seen yet can serve to stretch the higher-achieving students. They struggle through a question and come up with a reasonable answer, enriching their learning. I give the average students a couple of hints, "Hey guys, in the future if you see a problem like this, you might want to try this . . ."

We have to be careful when exposing students to skills we haven't covered. Lower-achieving students can become frustrated quickly, so be sure to mix in questions that everyone should be able to answer at least two or three days out of the week. And be sure to tell them, "Now, this is a question on the test." The entire class gains confidence and begins to think, "Hey, we can do this stuff!" Items that cover objectives the students haven't seen could also be assigned for groups, or even an entire class, to work on.

A correctly paced assessment calendar will allow you to build learning progressively throughout the year. Don't call in the fire brigade if a student scores zero out of four the first time she sees the objective assessed. Test the objective again later in the week and then again the next week. If needed, you can place her in Tier 2 remediation and then move her out of it when she masters the skill.

By slowly building throughout the year, we can monitor individual students and ensure that our remediation is successful. Using daily short assessments and more comprehensive intermediate tests at appropriate intervals allow us to keep an eye on the power objectives.

Following a well-planned format allows you as a teacher to make sure you are covering the most important material. You can then take control of your calendar and never have to feel you are surrendering to the standards.

Ask the Right Types of Questions

Although I will be covering the topic extensively throughout this book, I also feel compelled to mention the need to properly align classroom assessments with the item type and knowledge level of the test. The test should not be a surprise to your students. They should see practice items during the year that look exactly like the test in format, length, question type, proportion of standards, and level of difficulty.

State departments of education do a good job communicating not only the number of items on the test taken from each standard, but also on the type of question and the level of knowledge assessed. Find out the information and don't frustrate yourself or your students by spending too much time on questions that are too difficult or that don't look like those they will see on the test.

I like this school because they are putting
smarts in our heads.
– Kerri Lynn, 1st grade

Chapter 4

THE TIMER EFFECT

An Application Strategy

Overcoming the Power of the Internal and External Clocks

The Internal Timer

Is the test your students take timed? States have different guidelines regarding tests. Some are timed, some aren't, and some have certain portions timed. If your test is timed, stop and think a bit. Do your students ever run out of time? Your answer is most likely no. Very rarely does a student actually run out of time on the test.

If no one ever runs out of time, then is the test a timed test? It is, but maybe not in the way we normally think about timers. Whether or not the state puts a time limit on the test, a timer effect is always in play. There is a clock on the wall, but it's not the timer.

So what is the timer in your room?

The ***internal timer*** at work in your students is the speed of the other students sitting around them.

The timer at work in your room has different effects on students. Some might look around and see others finishing quickly and resign themselves to play the Christmas tree or Guitar Hero™ games with their answer sheets— you know, filling in the dots to create a Christmas tree or a pattern for a cool song just so they don't finish last. The timer might cause other students to feel the pressure to get the answers and move on, accepting good enough for their efforts.

Some students have no understanding of how much time they should spend on a given question. We know that some questions are easy and some are hard, but many students have no concept of how to allocate their time on each one.

Remember Steven from the first two chapters? His goal is just not to get done; he has to finish *first*. One teacher in Ohio told me, "Herman, I have three kids in my room just like that. It drives me crazy because they are always racing each other to finish first."

Whether or not a student is racing to finish first, the timer effect is still at work. When those first few students begin to finish and close their test booklets, most of the other students begin to feel that they have spent all the time on the test that they should have. Some might even be sitting there thinking, "Oh, please don't let me be the last one to finish." You can readily recognize that the timer in your room isn't the clock; it's the other students in the room.

An Exercise

I want to lead you through an exercise I do in my workshops so you can understand the effect of the internal timer. I tell the teachers that I will be asking them some easy questions after they read the short passage at the top of the next page. Additionally, I let them know they will be timed according to the first person finished. "Look up at me and smile when you are finished, and I will announce to the group that all of you have 15 seconds left."

This is an activity easily adapted to the grade level you teach. You can change the reading level, or you might use a number of math problems with the second person finished plus two minutes as the timer.

Jason loves to attend Scout camp in the summer. The camp is held the entire second week of July at Weller Lake, and he has been every year since he was six years old. This July will be especially fun because Jason hopes to complete all the steps to achieve his first-class rank during the camp. This summer will also be fun for another reason. Jason and his cousin Ethan will both be turning thirteen. Ethan's dad is Jason's Uncle Eric, and he has promised to take both boys for a week-long camping trip to Colorado to celebrate their birthdays! Now Jason has learned that the only vacation week Uncle Eric has is during the second week in July. That is the same week of his Scout camp! Is Jason going to have to choose between the two fun things to do? No one has talked to Jason yet about what *he* wants. Isn't there something that can be done so he can enjoy both?

After finishing the exercise, I like to have a honest conversation with teachers, asking two reflective questions:

1. How did you begin reading? Did you start out reading more slowly, underlining phrases mentally since you knew there would be questions? Or did you start out reading more quickly since you aren't a fast reader, and you wanted to make sure you finished?

2. What did you do when I called 15 seconds? Did you change the way you were reading? Did you speed up to make sure you finished, or did you go back over the passage to make sure you knew the answer to any question I might ask?

A timed exercise like this one causes us to feel empathy for our children. As we have a conversation, most teachers admit they felt some stress when they heard I was going to ask some questions. They started out slowly, knowing a test was at the end, but they sped up when I called 15 seconds.

I always ask, "For those of you who didn't get done—how did you feel?" One man was especially honest when he yelled out, "I felt stupid!" Think about that response. We as adults feel all the emotions of anxiety, uneasiness, and lack of confidence when taking a timed test over an elementary reading passage.

Just imagine the effect on twelve-year-old Alana as she opens her test booklet. Alana feels the timer at work. She glances over at Steven, not to cheat, but just to see how far he is on his booklet. She says to herself, "Why am I not turning my pages as fast as Steven? I need to speed up."

Student Responses to the Timer Problem

The timer effect causes students to have different responses. I've mentioned Steven, with the want-to-be-the-first problem. The effect might cause another student to say, "Hey, I'm not such a great student after all. Here's one part where I can go quickly and get done, and at least I'll look smart." In actual practice, because we seldom give students immediate feedback from test results, if any at all, they can easily play the Guitar Hero™ game and be done with the test.

The timer effect causes many students to fall into a rhythm of answering questions. Whether it's an easy question or a hard one doesn't matter. They merely fall into a pattern of spending the same amount of time on each question.

Other students might flip-flop the strategy a bit. When they see an easy question, they speed up to save some time for the hard ones. Don't we want them to speed up when they can save time? Not really. Remember the test probably isn't timed to begin with, so they won't run out of time. Students can easily make a simple mistake on a question in order to hurry past it. We need to teach them to be very thorough, checking answers even on easy questions, and being sure before moving on.

Fixing the Timer Problem

We can use several techniques to help fix the timer problem. First, I think having open and honest conversations with students about the test and hearing their responses to it is vital. We can empower students in many ways by giving them information, test-taking strategies, and tips to boost their performance. In the process, they gain self-confidence as we equip them. That increased confidence will naturally begin to improve test scores.

Have a Conversation With Your Students

I think it would be entirely appropriate to have the same conversation about the reading passage with students that I have with teachers. Again, you can easily adapt the exercise to other grade levels and subjects. I've done the same exercise with math teachers, putting a different problem on each page. As they turn pages completing the problems, I see the same type of responses, indicating the same emotions that are present with a reading exercise.

We know that in any 12-step program the first step is to admit we have a problem. Exercises like these with students allow them to understand what type of test taker they are, in effect, to recognize what their problem is.

Be prepared to have some powerful conversations with students when you do this exercise. My conversations with thousands of teachers have become quite predictable. Some will say they read slowly for detail. They are generally the fast readers. Others say, "We read fast because we are normally slow readers." Seeing the connection to your classroom is easy. You see some students read slowly for detail, while others speed up to make sure they get through the material.

Giving Them Strategies

The answer to the second question is very revealing. "What did you do when you heard there were only fifteen seconds left?" People say they rushed, their anxiety level went up, they forgot what they had read, etc.

Make that connection to your classroom. We know that no one during a high-stakes test says ready, set, go, and no one tells the class when they have only 10 seconds left. But the reality is that the timer sets in when that child in your room hears the one next to him turning the page. Of course, that child turning the page may not be any smarter. She might be playing the Christmas tree game, but the timer has already begun to tick for the conscientious student.

A student has the feeling that everyone around her is finishing the test, so she speeds up, when actually every teacher in the building would want her to slow down, take her time, and mark the answers correctly. A fatigue factor might also be in play as the student moves through the test. Whatever the cause, clearly the timer effect is an enormous issue for test takers.

Sometimes teachers inadvertently highlight the timer effect with practices that have unintended consequences. For example, I've seen teachers look around and say, "Hey, guys, it looks like we're all done. Let's pick up the test books and go out for an extra recess." What was the intended effect of the teacher's practice? Of course, she wanted to reward her children for working hard on the test, but what message did she send to her class?

Teacher Story

A math teacher told me that he and his fellow class-mates in a graduate course had completed a study in which they developed a test for middle school students. All the problems on the test were at the same level of difficulty, but they discovered that the students taking the test scored 30% lower on the last one-third of the test than on the first one-third of the test.

I can think of two reasons for students to score 30% lower on the last one-third of the test: either they thought they ran out of time or they ran out of gas. You can give them strategies from this chapter to help alleviate the time problem. If your students grow weary before the end of the test, have them take a break, close their books, move around, stretch, do a yoga exercise, or whatever you need to get their energy level back up.

A good friend of mine told me about a recent hunter safety course he completed. The participants had to score a certain level on a test in order to earn certification. Before passing out the test booklets, the instructor held up a prize and announced, "The first five people who get 100% on the test will get one of these." What was the intended effect? He wanted to increase quality on the test, but the unintended consequence was to motivate everyone to speed up and finish the test as fast as they could. At least they sped up until the first five people turned their tests in!

Teacher Story

In a recent workshop in Kansas, a teacher had an epiphany as I discussed unintended consequences. She raised her hand and said, "I can't believe what I've been doing. When the kids are done with the test, I allow them to play games on the computer. I just realized that I'm unintentionally giving them an incentive to hurry and complete the test without being careful with their answers."

Some states say no reading after the test, while others tell students that they can take out a reading book after they finish. Be careful to follow the guidelines prescribed by your state but think about the unintended consequences of certain practices. You know your population, and you know best what your students need in order perform well.

Practice with a Timer

A timer tends to stress all of us, especially students. So why should we practice using a timer if it stresses them? I understand the reluctance, but if students are going to face stress in a timed situation, isn't it better to deal with that stress before they sit down in a high-stakes setting?

I recommend using a countdown timer prior to the standardized test. I wouldn't use it every day or even every week, but I want to get students accustomed to using it and working in a timed setting. For example, you might set a ten-minute timer at the front of your room and give the students a short quiz. Tell them, "Kids, when you finish answering each question, look up here and see how much time you have left. Record it in the blank beside your answer." An example is shown below.

Question	Answer	Time Remaining
1.	A B C D	_____
2.	A B C D	_____
3.	A B C D	_____
4.	A B C D	_____
5.	A B C D	_____

Students then begin the test. For example, a student would answer one question, look up, and see 9:02 remaining. He would write the time down and move on to the next question, thinking it's an easy one. He would answer it, record the time left, and so on. Of course, Steven will say, "Seven minutes and 30 seconds—oh yeah, a new record!"

Strategies to Address the Time Issue

Using a timer in formative settings before the test gives your students a sense of what to expect. It also allows you to have substantial conversations with them. For example, you can ask them what they were doing during the 58 seconds they took to answer the first question. If they can't tell you what they were doing, then you can be ready to give them a strategy.

When Steven finishes in seven minutes, do you tell him to slow down or nag him a bit? Instead, you could show him a video of a gazelle who ran too fast and was eaten. (The link to the *Stupid Gazelle* video can be found in the Appendix.) You can then say, "Steven, what is going to happen to that gazelle? He's going to be eaten, isn't he? Now you have to slow down so this test doesn't eat you. You have to do it, Steven. Will you slow down for me? Will you do it for this class?"

You can provide Steven strategies, such as giving him a Jolly Rancher™ to suck on while he is taking the test, telling him you don't want him finished until the candy is gone. Another strategy that I will discuss in more detail in Chapter 9 is using a test passport, with one of the stamps in the passport being wise use of time which the student must earn in order to attend the party after the test.

The candy is symbolic of whatever you are going to use to help your students pace themselves. You can give the speeder a Jolly Rancher™ and tell him not to be finished with the test until he finishes with the candy. Then give him a star mint and tell him to not finish that candy until he has gone back and checked his answers.

What about Alana, who is too deliberate? She is so conscientious that she takes too much time on each question until she is about to run out of time, and then she speeds up and guesses on the last third of the test. Use the candy as a reverse strategy. She should be at a certain point on the test when she finishes the Jolly Rancher™. Again, the candy is merely a symbol of any strategy you might put in place.

Testing Tip

Several times I've been asked whether displaying a timer while students are taking a timed standardized test is acceptable. In checking with most states, I haven't found one that does not allow a teacher to display a timing device during the test, but I strongly advise you to consult your testing manual before using the practice.

It's easy to make a buck. It's a lot harder to make a difference.
– Tom Brokaw

Time Management

Another effect of the timer is the tendency for students to rush through the easy questions to save time for the more difficult ones. But remember, every question on the test has been field tested. That means the question won't even get on the test unless enough students get it wrong. Standardized tests really have no "gimme" questions.

You want your students to spend enough time on every question to make sure their answers are correct, so you need to give them some strategies to slow down and prove their answer to themselves before moving on. You might have them go back to the source material, whether it's a question or a reading source. Maybe they can solve the problem a second way. On a multiple choice test they can take some time to reduce the possibilities. They might say to themselves, "I know the answer is (a), but I'll take a few minutes to go back and eliminate (b), (c), and (d)."

You can also teach students to use estimation strategies. On a math question, they can first determine if the answer will be large, small, positive or negative. They might think about the correct label or what the orientation of the graph would be. Estimation isn't only a math strategy. In science and social studies it might mean to sit and think about the question before answering and predict what form the answer will take.

Language arts teachers can instruct students to be thinking about the possible questions as they read through the prompt. Above all, practice questions during the year should be in the same format as the ones students will see on the standardized test.

Teaching Tip

Eight Ways to Solve a Word Problem

1. Find a Pattern
2. Make a Table
3. Work Backwards
4. Guess and Check
5. Draw a Picture
6. Make a List
7. Write a Number Sentence
8. Use Logical Reasoning

Preview the Test

Another key skill for students to master in time management is to preview the test effectively. Many students typically open the test booklet and begin working from the first question with no thought toward organizing their efforts. We know that no standardized test, from third grade reading to the ACT, organizes questions in levels of difficulty. Training students to approach a test with a plan of attack as early as possible in their educational careers makes sense.

I must be very clear that previewing the test DOES NOT mean getting the test booklets out on Friday to go over what the students will see on Monday. Nor does it mean giving the students questions that read like the actual test questions, with a minor change in wording.

My premise is that a quick-review strategy will raise scores. Remember the study that found students missed 30% more of the questions on the last one-third of the test? I'm not sure if they ran out of time or ran out of gas, but as the teacher, I would want to make sure that they are first answering the questions they definitely know.

Teach your students how to preview a section of the test and figure out which questions they know. It is imperative that they understand to preview the SECTION only; they cannot move on to other sections. Teach them to skip a difficult problem and come back to it after making sure they have correct answers on the other questions.

Testing Tip

I'm asked many times if students previewing the test sections this way is legal. Absolutely! In fact, the test booklets tell students to skip the harder questions and come back to them.

What if students take too much time previewing the test? We've already established that the vast majority of students will never run out of time. Again, even if they do run out of time, don't you want to be sure they are first answering the questions they know? After observing practice sessions, you can work privately with the students who are being too deliberate and spending too much time previewing.

Some students might need symbols to help them preview the test and mark the questions.

Sample Symbols

☺	I am sure I know how to do this problem
+	I am fairly sure I know how to do this problem
F	I should use my formula sheet on this problem
C	I should use a calculator on this problem
L	I must remember to label this answer

Practicing this strategy throughout the year is important. On the day of the test, you may give only the instructions stated in the tester's manual. Otherwise, it wouldn't be a standardized test. You must teach these strategies ahead of time, so that students understand this is just how we do things in this class.

While this preview strategy doesn't work so well on language arts test passages, you will find it very successful on a math, social studies, or grammar/spelling test.

Imagine the power of a high school senior using preview strategies as she takes the ACT. She will most likely run out of time if she opens the test and begins working in order from the first question. Then she has no choice but to play the Christmas tree game for the remaining portion of the test and surely miss some question that she could have completed correctly. Compare that scenario to opening the test, quickly previewing the questions and marking the ones she knows, pacing herself as she moves through it.

Before moving on from this discussion, I want to give you an idea a teacher shared with us in a workshop session. She uses the acronym PIRATES for her students.

PIRATES

P *Preview* the test and *Prepare* for success.

I *Inspect* the *Instructions* on every question.

R *Read* the source material, *Remember* the information, and *Reduce* the possibilities.

A *Answer* or *Abandon*.

T *Turn* back to the ones you know how to do.

E *Every* question is answered. We *Estimate* or give it an *Educated* guess.

S *Scan* the test, going back to make sure everything looks like it should.

The internal timer is a huge issue on tests. Help your students learn about their own approach to the timer effect and give them strategies to manage their time as they take the test.

Blessed is the man who, having nothing to say, abstains from giving us wordy evidence of the fact.
  – George Eliot

Chapter 5

THE QUESTION–ANSWER RELATIONSHIP (QAR)

Strategies in
Reading

Defining the QAR

The previous chapter outlines the powerful conversations we can have with students when they practice taking a timed test. From those conversations we can give them strategies to make more efficient use of their time. One strategy I find very helpful is the *Question/Answer Relationship* as developed by Raphael (1986).

Raphael created Question-Answer Relationships (QAR) as a way to help students realize that the answers they seek relate to the type of question asked. The approach encourages them to be strategic about their search for answers based on the type of question. Even more important is understanding where the answer will come from.

Teaching QARs to students begins with helping them understand the core notion that when confronted with a question, the answer will come either from the text or from what they know. These are the Core Categories, which Raphael calls

1. In the Book
2. In My Head

Becoming comfortable with these simple distinctions will help students move to the next level of understanding question types. Raphael divides In The Book into two QAR types: Right There and Think and Search. He also divides In My Head into two QAR types: Author and You and On my Own.

A graphic organizer at the top of the next page helps us understand the scheme.

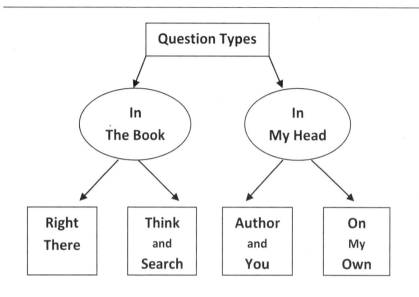

Raphael, 1986

Right There Questions require you to go back to the passage and find the correct information to answer the question. The answer is in the text, and if someone pointed at it, you would say it's right there! Right There questions sometimes include the words, "How many . . .," "According to the passage . . .," Who is . . .," or "What is . . ."

Think and Search Questions usually require you to think about how ideas or information in the passage relate to each other. You might have to look back at several different sentences or paragraphs in the passage to find the answer. Then you will have to think about how the information or ideas fit together. Think and Search questions many times include the words, "The main idea of the passage . . .," "Compare . . .," or "What caused . . ."

Author and You Questions require you to use ideas and information not stated directly in the passage. Even though the answer is not in the text, you still need information the author has given you, combined with what you already know. These questions require you to think about what you have read and formulate your own ideas or opinions. Author and You questions might include the words, "The passage suggests . . .," 'The author implies . . ., "or "The speaker's attitude . . ."

On My Own Questions require you to use your background knowledge about a topic. Many times you don't even have to read the text to be able to answer it. This type of question does not usually appear on tests of reading comprehension because it does not require you to refer to the passage. Questions sometimes include the words, "In your opinion . . .," "Based on your experience . . .," or "Think about someone/something you know . . ."

Think again about the reading passage from Chapter 4 and look at the various question types that might be asked.

Jason loves to attend Scout camp in the summer. The camp is held the entire second week of July at Weller Lake, and he has been every year since he was six years old. This July will be especially fun because Jason hopes to complete all the steps to achieve his first-class rank during the camp.

This summer will also be fun for another reason. Jason and his cousin Ethan will both be turning thirteen. Ethan's dad is Jason's Uncle Eric, and he has promised to take both boys for a week-long camping trip to Colorado to celebrate their birthdays! Now Jason has learned that the only vacation week Uncle Eric has is during the second week in July. That is the same week of his Scout camp! Is Jason going to have to choose between the two fun things to do? No one has talked to Jason yet about what *he* wants. Isn't there something that can be done so he can enjoy both?

Some possible questions could be

Right There

1. Where is the Scout camp that Jason wants to attend this summer?
2. What is Jason's cousin's name?

Think and Search

1. How old is Jason right now?
2. Does Jason like to go camping?

Author and You

1. Who might Jason want to talk to about his problem?

On My Own

1. In what ways can going camping be exciting?

Right There Questions

A question like "Where is the Scout camp located?" is, of course, a right there question because the answer is . . . well, it's right there. It's what most kids would call an easy question, and it's one that they will many times answer quickly and then move on to the next question. But in that haste, they can make some critical mistakes. Do you want them to answer the question from memory or glance quickly over the text and possibly see *Colorado* instead of *Weller Lake?*

We want students to ignore the internal timer, slow down, and prove even the easy answers to themselves. A common way to prove an answer on a reading comprehension test is for students to go back to the text and underline the key information that helped them arrive at the answer.

On the formative tests leading up to the high-stakes test, you might want to give your students one point for the right answer, another point for underlining where they found it, and maybe even a third point for writing where they got the answer. Of course, our Steven might figure out that he can underline everything to make sure he gets the point. So I establish the 3/10 rule: underline no more than three words in a row and no more than ten words in a paragraph.

A question asked in the right way often
points to its own answer.
– Edward Hodnett

Think and Search Questions

A think and search question such as "How old is Jason right now?" requires students to deduce information from the text. They need to know that Jason is turning 13 this summer, and that makes him 12 currently. They can also prove their answer to the question by underlining the passages in the text that they used to figure out the correct answer.

Many times think and search questions deal with the main idea or the conflict in the story. We want to make sure our students have plenty of practice to use strategies in the formative assessments during the year.

Author and You Questions

An author and you question can cause a girl like Melissa to become frustrated and lose confidence in herself. Answers to questions such as "What do you think is going to happen?" or "What does the author think?" are not obvious in the text. Melissa is a slow reader and a teacher-pleaser, so she will read and reread, trying to find the answer. But the answer just isn't there, and frustration sets in. Our students need to understand clearly that sometimes they will encounter a question that doesn't have the answer in the text, so they don't need to spend a lot of time trying to prove their answer to a question like that.

Remember the on my own questions don't have the answer in the text at all, so they will never appear on a reading comprehension test. You will find them instead as a prompt on a writing test.

Stray Marks on the Test

A question regarding stray marks in the test booklets invariably arises when we talk about underlining text. A graphite mark on one page can possibly be transferred when the facing page is turned, resulting in a grading error. The same holds for highlighters, which can bleed through the page and bond the graphite to the paper.

Keep in mind that a discussion about stray marks must first consider what type of test your students are taking. Stray marks won't matter if a human scores the test, such as a writing assessment or short-answer constructed response questions. On those, even if stray marks transfer or bleed through, they will not cause a grading error.

The stray marks become an issue to consider if a machine does the scoring, as in the case of most multiple choice tests. Testing companies tell us that putting a stray mark anywhere on the answer sheet is a risky practice. Will the test be thrown out if there is a stray mark? No, but it's a risky practice because of the possibility of the graphite transferring to another page.

As a teacher, you need to decide whether the benefit of your students using strategies such as underlining outweigh the necessity of erasing the marks. In most states the district testing coordinator is responsible to ensure that all stray marks are erased, so I encourage you to consult him or her. Can you have students erase? Are you prepared as a teacher or a building to have an erasing party if they don't erase?

Discover in those formative assessments throughout the year if your class benefits from underlining, or maybe even which students benefit most. Take one test with underlining and one without. If there is a difference, I would go to the testing coordinator and be prepared to erase stray marks.

Again, please check with your district testing coordinator for further guidance regarding stray marks.

Testing Tip

What would your students consider a bad grade? 90%? 80%? 70%? 60%? We many times condition students to equate successful performance with a percentage. How many words can a student miss on a 20-question spelling test and be considered successful? Maybe three or four at the most.

How many questions can your students miss on the standardized test and be considered proficient? The answer varies from state to state, but many states set the benchmark at 50% or less. With that benchmark, a student can miss half of the questions and still be proficient. Do your students know that? Do you know the level of proficiency expected in your state?

I encourage you to examine closely the expectations outlined by your state. The Appendix lists the websites for all state departments of education.

We set our students up for performance, and some high achievers are devastated if they receive an A- on their report card. But very few will receive a score as high as an A- on the standardized test. They need to know that. A completely different scale governs the test than the one we use in most schools.

Have you taken the GRE? I remember walking out of the GRE feeling like an idiot, yet I received the results and discovered I did pretty well. Our students think they have to get most of the questions correct to be successful. Many of them are taking the test thinking, "Oh no, I'm getting half of the questions wrong. I'm failing." Yet 50% is proficient in many states.

Let your students know exactly what to expect. Maybe you can practice with a test that looks like the real one. The students wouldn't even have to take the test, but merely go over the questions and mark the ones they think they know how to answer correctly. Then you can ask them, "You know how to do 20 of the questions? You have an excellent shot of doing well on this test." You can help your students build confidence and greatly reduce anxiety as the test day approaches.

You can get all A's and still flunk life.
– Walker Percy

Chapter 6

TEST ITEM TYPES

Maximizing Efforts on
All Types of Items

Understanding Item Types

Regardless of the specific measurement model or scoring approach, all of the processes used to assess student performance begin at the item level.

Only two types of items appear on standardized tests:

1. Items that are scored by a computer
2. Items that are scored by a human

Computer-Scored Items

Multiple choice items comprise the majority of high-stakes test questions and are graded exclusively by computer. Some states and/or testing companies refer to these items as selected response items.

Scoring on these items is straightforward; students select from the available options, only one of which is the correct response. Students who select only the correct option receive a score of one (1), and students who select one of the incorrect options or did not respond receive a score of zero (0).

The high-stakes tests in some states consist exclusively of multiple choice or selected response items. You are very familiar with multiple choice items, such as the example found at the top of the next page.

The most significant word
in teacher is "each."
– Robert DeBruyn

Which of these best describe the main conflict in the passage?

a. A boy's desire to win and his love for his dog
b. The narrator's struggle to survive in challenging weather
c. A boy's wish for success and his friendship with a competitor
d. The narrator's belief in his dog's ability and his doubts about himself

Human-Scored Items

Humans score items generally referred to as short answer or constructed response items. They use two techniques in scoring these types of items:

1. Holistic scoring
2. Analytic scoring

Holistic Scoring

When using holistic scoring, scorers review a response for an overall or whole impression and assign a score. A holistically scored language arts item usually takes the form of a writing assignment following a prompt that is typically based on a previous text. Items of this sort in science or mathematics require the student to gather information given in the text and apply a series of steps to arrive at a correct answer. Students are many times asked to present the data in a graphic organizer, such as in a bar graph and/or table.

An example of a holistically scored language arts item is at the top of the next page.

Writing Prompt

Think about a problem that many teenagers face today. Write a paper to share with your class in which you describe the problem and explain how it might be resolved.

Analytic scoring

Most analytically scored items have two parts, requiring the student to answer the question correctly *and* also adequately explain the answer. Items of this sort typically are worth more than one point and the scorer assigns the student either zero (0), one (1), two (2), or more points according to specific criteria published in a scoring guide. An example of an analytically scored item is shown below.

Study the number pattern. Write the next two numbers that continue the pattern.

$$3, \quad 4, \quad 6, \quad 9, \quad \underline{\quad\quad}, \quad \underline{\quad\quad}$$

On the lines below, write the rule for the pattern

_____

_____

With both types of constructed response scoring, the testing companies provide extensive training and practice to the scorers. They evaluate writing and/or the problem-solving process, not writers. Companies train scorers to ignore extraneous factors such as neatness and instead to focus on the strengths of responses rather than the weaknesses. During the scoring process, periodic quality-control checks are in place to ensure that scorers are evaluating responses consistently.

I strongly suggest that you check with your district testing coordinator or your state department of education to know the format of the test that your students will be taking. To best prepare your students, you must first know the scoring guides used for each type of test item.

Scoring Guide Formula

The sample scoring guide on the next page shows how a student's answer might be scored on a constructed response item. Look at the scoring guide closely. This particular scoring guide assigns two points for a "complete and accurate" answer. Make sure you and your students completely understand how the points are assigned on your state's test.

School need not be merely a place where big people who are learned teach little people who are learners.
– Roland Barth

Scoring Guidelines

Points	Student Response
2 points	Points awarded for a complete and accurate statement Response indicates the main problem AND Response indicates a text-based solution Note: The problem may be embedded in the solution, or the solution may be embedded in the problem.
1 point	Point awarded for a partially complete or somewhat inaccurate statement. Response correctly identifies the main problem without providing a text-based solution OR Response identifies a text-based solution without correctly stating the main problem.
0 points	No point awarded if a statement is non-existent or completely inaccurate. Response does not contain the correct answer listed above, is incomplete, irrelevant, or blank. The response shows no understanding of the task.

Students need plenty of practice during the year with items of this sort. Remember we want to practice like we play. I believe the most important word in the scoring guide is *and*. Without understanding that they need to list both parts to the answer clearly, students can easily give a partial response and move on to the next question.

I suggest developing a scoring guide formula to help your students see the need for a complete answer. An example of a formula from this scoring guide might be

$$1MP + 1TS = 2P$$

That is, one main problem plus one text-based solution equals two points. Students can see easily that one main problem with no text-based solution equals only one point, or vice versa. They can practice with items of this type all year, using the scoring guide to grade themselves or peer grade to get a complete understanding of the expectations.

Spelling and Grammar

Look back at the scoring guide. Does the student need to be able to spell correctly in order to get two points? How about paragraphing? Periods and capitalization? No, spelling and grammar don't count on analytically scored items. These types of questions are evaluating only the student's ability to comprehend information from text and express it clearly.

In fact, I've talked to teachers who have scored these tests. They tell me their teacher hearts break to see a beautifully written answer, using all the lines, and with correct spelling and grammar but not answering the question correctly. The student gets a zero. Then they see a paper that looks like the kid vomited on it. It's smudged, messy, and maybe the kid didn't even use vowels. It may look like a text message, but as long as they can tell what the student means, he or she gets the points.

Spelling and grammar don't count on this type of question! Does it matter in math and science? Of course it doesn't. As a principal in the building, I wouldn't get on the intercom and announce, "OK, students, don't worry about spelling, grammar, and handwriting on this test." As a teacher, I wouldn't even announce it to my class because remember we want to improve test scores without losing our soul. Spelling, grammar, and handwriting are essential skills we want our students to master, but they won't improve scores on this portion of the test.

Instead, I might pull one student aside who struggles. Do I want him to focus on good sentence structure or putting ideas down correctly? For this test I want him to focus on getting his ideas down. I can pull him aside and say, "Troy, let me tell you a secret about this part of the test." Knowing this helps Troy better prepare for such items.

Many schools have a boot camp or survivor type of activity leading up to the test. Maybe your school concentrates on preparing your students for the test for two weeks before the actual event. In any case, don't stress about spelling and grammar in that period and don't demand it from students on these types of questions. At that time you want them to be focusing on the skills that will raise their scores.

Genius without education is like silver in the mine.
– Benjamin Franklin

Teacher Story

One teacher told me her students practice the constructed response questions all year long in both language arts and math. She gives them the scoring guide and thoroughly explains it to them. Early in the year, she also provides sample answers to score. Then they compare their scoring to the actual score given.

As they become familiar with the process, she allows them to score themselves on items similar to ones on the test. They even do peer review on items completed by other students in the class. She expressed amazement at how quickly they become expert scorers.

Never have ideas about children, and never
have ideas for them.
–George Orwell

Answer All Parts of the Question

Students tend to have two problems when answering constructed response questions. Either they don't answer all parts of the question or if they do, they run out of space in the answer booklet. Look at the sample question below that follows a reading passage.

Explain Marco's first reaction to the smells in the air as he enters his father's shop. Then, identify three specific smells that he notices afterward.

Notice the first part of the question, "Explain Marco's first reaction . . .," and the second part, "identify three specific smells . . ." Students need to be trained to recognize two distinct parts to the question. A scoring guide formula might be

$$1R + 3S = 4P$$

That is, one reaction to the smells plus three specific smells equals four points.

Remember, a text would accompany a reading comprehension item such as this one. Students would first read the text, and then refer to it as they answer the questions. One strategy might be to instruct them to underline the first part of the question with one line and underline the answer to that part with one line in the text. Then they underline the second part of the question with two lines and go to the text to underline the answer with two lines. In this instance, they would be underlining all three examples that they find.

Test writers call the first part of a question of this type the *description*. The description could be a question such as "What's the setting of the story?" or "What was the main idea?" The next part of the question is called the *example*. In this case, that would be to describe the three smells.

The Space Issue

A space issue arises with many students when they answer a question of this type. Let's suppose five lines are in the test booklet to answer the question. The answer should be as long as necessary to answer the question correctly, but what happens if a student runs out of space?

Sometimes we teach students to restate the question, but they don't get any points on this test for restating it. I still think it's a great strategy to use in the classroom, but what happens if they spend three lines restating the question, and then a line and a half for the description portion of the question? With only a half line to spare, they say, "I must be done!"

Different students have different problems with the space issue. Melissa and Alana would have a dilemma if they ran out of room, but Steven will never run out of room! So what do we tell Melissa and Alana? Let me tell you the truth first, and then I will tell you what I would say to them in actual practice.

What If a Student Continues below the Line?

Although procedures vary, most states have the completed student booklets returned to the testing company for scoring. A machine called a slicer first cuts off the bound edge. Every page has a barcode to ensure that students' answers are tracked properly. After slicing, a computer scans each page. That means the scorers don't look at a student's actual page when they sit down to grade the test. Instead, they are looking at a picture of the page.

The scorers sit at a table looking at a computer screen, scoring maybe only one item all day. Number 15, for example, comes across the screen one after another. Actually, they become extremely fast and accurate with the task.

Scorers tell me, "Herman, we've been told that whatever shows up on the computer screen can be scored." Well, the whole page shows up! It's the same on the math test. The student's answer will be scored even if he or she works outside of the box.

I can't assure you that *every* state follows these guidelines, but I can tell you that every scorer I've talked to from a large number of states has told me the same thing: they score whatever they can see on the page.

What Do We Tell the Kids?

I never tell my students that their answers will be scored no matter where they show up on the page. I don't want the scorers to have to look all over the place, finding one part of the answer here and another part over there. That creates the chance of the scorer missing an answer if he or she has to look all over the page. Also, I want my students to learn and practice skills to organize thoughts and present them in an orderly fashion.

You can tell your students, "Now when you are answering a question and you get to the bottom of the page, make sure you answer it completely." Maybe they can double up and get two lines in there or neatly draw extra lines at the bottom to extend their space. But continuing to write until they completely answer the question is vitally important. One teacher told me she asks her class how long the answer should be, and they answer in unison, "As long as it takes!"

In those formative assessments all year long, you can train students to be succinct by focusing on only the information the question requires to help them get their answers in the space provided.

Testing Tip

Numbering answers is an excellent strategy to teach students. One scorer told me "Every kid who uses this strategy gets every answer right." I'm not ready to accept that *every* student gets it right, but I'll say that most students who use this strategy get most of the answers correct.

Look at the sample of a student's response to the item on page 103.

1. No place smells anything like it. If you close your eyes and try to pick out what it is that you're sniffing, you're only going to get confused.
2. I get a sniff of new tires.
3. Then there was a smell of oil and grease.
4. Then I could smell the onions on Dad's cheeseburger as he looked up at me and smiled.

"Explain Marco's reaction . . .," is part one. Then "identify three . . .," are parts two, three and four. Students can write what they want on the test, including numbering. Notice that in the sample response above, the student numbered the parts 1, 2, 3, and 4, and received full credit for the answer. This is an easy strategy to teach kids, and ensures they are answering all parts of the question. You can tell them they are proving their answer. Students must also understand that copying directly from the text in their answers is acceptable.

Testing Tip

The *insurance* strategy always works for the example part of the response. Students receive no penalty for giving more examples than the instructions call for, even if one of the given examples is wrong. Suppose the instructions call for two examples from the text, and a student gives three examples for insurance. She receives full credit if the scorer finds two correct examples out of the three that she gave.

The insurance strategy never works for the description part of the question because it has only one right answer. For example, the student contradicts herself if the question calls for the setting of the story and she answers both Alaska and Orlando.

A young child is, indeed, a true scientist, just one big question mark. What? Why? How? I never cease to marvel at the recurring miracle of growth, to be fascinated by the mystery and wonder of this brave enthusiasm.
— Victoria Wagner

At the risk of being redundant, let me highlight some tips from this chapter:

Constructed Response (Analytic Scoring)

- Students don't receive a score for spelling and grammar on this type of response (unless specifically stated).
- Use a system of underlining to ensure that students are using text-based examples. Be sure that you do this all year long. Give an equal number of points for the students writing their answers, as well as for showing where they found them.
- When providing practice for students on these types of questions, be sure that you are simulating testing conditions. Many teachers use these types of questions on comprehension tests to get students in the habit of not looking in the source material to support their answers.
- When practicing for these types of questions in math, students should have a formula sheet if they normally have one during the standardized test.
- Many of the scoring guides in math will give one point for the correct process and one point for the correct answer. Scoring guides can help students understand why they must show all their work.
- Use of space is important on these types of questions. Students tend to give incomplete answers because they run out of space to write. Either teach

them that less is more or teach them to keep writing even if they run out of space.

- Restating the question is a powerful strategy to keep students focused on this type of question. However, they do not receive any points on the test for using this strategy.
- Students can use the insurance strategy when asked to give examples on this type of question.

When your mother is mad and asks, "Do I look stupid?"
it's best not to answer her.
– Megham, age 13

Chapter 7

GETTING ORGANIZED

The 4-Square Method

The Brain Dump

The SMART 7

The 4-Square Organizer

Teaching students to organize knowledge, ideas, or concepts into a coherent pattern is one of the most powerful strategies to increase performance and student achievement over time. Graphic organizers are instructional tools used to help students see the relationships among those ideas or information and to prepare to solve a problem, write, or speak.

Marzano (2001) feels that graphic organizers are the "most common way to help students generate nonlinguistic representation" (p. 75). He suggested that all graphic organizers be placed into six common patterns. For our discussion I want to focus on the classic 4-square organizer that is useful for both math and language arts.

Look at the organizer below. It's a simple method to help students stop, think about the problem, and organize information before beginning. Which of those four steps cost your students the most points on a standardized test?

Math 4-Square Organizer

What is the question? What solution does the problem ask for?	*What steps will need to be done* to arrive at the answer or solution?
Work the problem.	*Explain* what you did and why you did it.

Think about it a minute. Before reading on, go back and look carefully at the steps.

Many of us would say that the fourth step is the one our students struggle with the most. Explaining their work is a higher-order skill that requires students to know how to solve the problem. While explaining the work is a huge issue, scorers invariably tell me that students lose more points from the first step. If they can't understand what the question calls for, they don't know how to begin the problem. In reality, a multiple choice or short answer test doesn't ask the student to explain the work. Only states that require a performance event expect that level of inference.

Students should be able to solve problems at all levels of Depth of Knowledge (DOK). A sample DOK chart can be found in the Appendix. Practice those skills all year long, but for the purposes of preparing for the high-stakes test, focus your efforts on practicing skills that are in proportion to those that will show up on the test.

Mathematics is a subject so foundational that students are in trouble on the test if they don't have basic skills. For example, a sixth grader who shows up for the test and can't multiply is in trouble. Your formative assessments throughout the year should tell you the foundational portion of skills that your students don't know and give you the knowledge to make wise instructional decisions for your class.

To respond is positive; to react is negative.
– Zig Ziglar

Teacher Story

A seventh-grade teacher recently came to me in a workshop with an amen story. She said that two years ago she had the lowest-scoring class in the district in math. She was nervous, afraid that she might be fired, and she was desperately searching for some solutions. On her own she began to realize that her students simply couldn't identify the problem. They could for the most part solve the algorithms once they understood what the problem was asking for.

The students were struggling too much with seventh grade work, so she started below instructional level with fifth-grade problems. She didn't take the entire hour, just handing out one fifth-grade problem and having the students answer basic questions. She had them determine what the problem was asking for, what the solution would look like, if the answer would be a big number or a little number, what the units would be in the answer, etc.

She moved to sixth-grade problems when her class had mastered the skills with fifth-grade problems, and then to seventh-grade problems before the end of the year. The good news is that in one year she moved her students from the lowest scoring to the highest scoring class in the district.

Education is the transmission of civilization.
– Will Durant

Help Students Identify the Question

Students appear to have difficulty identifying the question in math for three main reasons:

1. The student is not able to read or is reading at least two grade levels below the level of the test.
2. The student struggles with the vocabulary on the test.
3. The student has difficulty differentiating between the types of problems on the test.

Every Teacher a Reading Teacher

Finding ELL students and English-speaking poor readers who can do the math but have difficulty reading the question is not uncommon. They know that 3 + 2 equals 5, but they can't get past the reading. What will be your focus in tutoring a child struggling to read? My opinion is that you should practice reading. The teacher might say, "But I'm a math teacher, not a reading teacher." I remind you that the title of this book is *Improving Student Test Scores*.

I understand that we can't all teach reading, but we are referring to a student who can do the math but struggles with the words. He or she needs help comprehending the question by possibly identifying key words that point to certain algorithms. A wise use of tutoring time, ELL or Title I intervention time, or just personal time working with the struggling reader in class, would be to focus on helping them identify those key words that point to certain algorithms.

Teaching Vocabulary

Many students struggle with vocabulary in math. Do they know that sum really means addition? What does the test mean when it asks them to decompose a number? Most states have a list of vocabulary words used on the test. Visit your state education department's webpage to find that list for your students. You can find a list of state webpages in the Appendix.

Spending as much time teaching some students how to identify key words and determine what is necessary to solve the problem can be as helpful as teaching them to actually solve the algorithm.

The key to vocabulary acquisition is to practice those words throughout the entire year. It's not helpful to give your students a list of fifty vocabulary words the week before the test. Use those words on assignments and tests throughout the year. Use the brain dump strategy discussed later in this chapter to help students remember the key vocabulary words. Practice like we play!

Differentiating between Question Types

Students have difficulty differentiating between types of questions because many times the high-stakes test is one of the first times they see a multiplicity of topics all mixed together. We tend to deliver math in units: first, addition; then subtraction; then units in geometry and geometry; and so on. Of course, the foundational nature of math requires some units to be taught sequentially.

But the standardized test never comes in units, nor is it organized by level of difficulty. Our children have a dilemma if this is the first time they see a jumble of different kinds of problems. The lack of organization makes shifting gears from one type of question to another very difficult for many students.

Testing Tip

Interestingly enough, we may need to turn to our first-grade teacher friends for strategies on helping students differentiate. In the upper grades we sometimes forget that it can become an issue. How does a first-grade teacher help students differentiate? They practice: "OK, kids, today we're going to learn the difference between an addition and a subtraction problem. Let's circle the addition problem and underline the subtraction problem."

Differentiating may not be a problem for every student, although I feel it's an issue for many. For some it may be *the* problem. When you practice identifying the question, make sure you also practice recognizing the question type.

Socrates didn't have an overhead projector. He asked questions that bothered people, and 3500 years later people are still talking about him.
-Hanoch McCarty

UPS, Check

I like to use the *UPS, Check* method with students. They can use the 4-square organizer: *Understand* the question, *Plan* your work, *Solve* the problem, and *Check* your answer.

Understand the Question	*Plan* Your Work
Solve the Problem	*Check* Your Answer

Articulating the plan is especially important for students. They need to talk about how many steps the problem will require, why it needs those steps, and what the answer will look like. On a constructed response item, you might want to teach students to number their steps or to use letters for steps if you don't want stray numbers on the answer sheet.

Another technique is to have students use a *work, what, why* chart in a double-t format:

Work	What	Why
4 + 3 = 7	"I added four plus three to get seven."	"It asked for how many in all."

The why is usually the hardest part for the students to answer. You might want to have a poster on the wall with sentence starters to help them. Sentence starters are a way to encourage students to write about the problems they tackled in a more concise and complete way.

Here are some sample sentence starters for math:

Sentence Starters for Math

1. I decided to . . . so that/because . . .
2. I noticed that . . .
3. I noticed a connection between . . .
4. When I looked . . .
5. Using the numbers in my table . . .
6. I tried . . .
7. This reminded me of . . .
8. I tested . . .
9. I wondered why . . .
10. This didn't work, so . . .
11. This worked, so . . .
12. I already know that . . ., so . . .
13. This is true because . . .

Distractors

Students need to understand the nature of *distractors* and their purpose on a multiple choice test. On any standardized test, the correct response and the three distractors are similar in length, syntax, or magnitude. Students should not be able to rule out a wrong answer solely because it looks different from other choices. Test writers create distractors so that students have to reason their way to the correct answer rather than simply identify incorrect choices.

Suppose a math question has four choices: a, b, c, and d. The correct answer would have the correct number and correct label. One good distractor would have the correct number but wrong label: inches instead of centimeters, for example. Another distractor might have the correct label but wrong number.

A very powerful distractor in math is one that is a correct answer on one of the steps of the problem. If the problem takes three steps, the distractor might be the answer to the second step. The student gets to that point in the process, sees that option as a choice, and marks the wrong answer. Practice finding the distractors on a multiple choice test with your students.

Teacher Story

I had a conversation with a teacher before a workshop began in which she was talking about students who don't answer all parts of the problem. "It drives me crazy when my kids don't do all the steps. They either stop too soon or pull the answer out of their heads," she said.

Later as we practiced the timer effect with the group, this teacher finished very quickly. This exercise had three multi-step math problems, and she answered the first step and neglected the second step on two of the three problems. The light bulb went on, and she said aloud, "That's exactly what is happening to my kids."

Give Your Students Strategies

Strategies are important to empower students and give them confidence as they take the test. For example, some students have difficulty memorizing multiplication tables. If a student can't remember that 4 times 3 equals 12, then teach him how to add 4 together 3 times. I like to say, "When in doubt, dot it out."

$$4 \times 3$$

$$
\begin{matrix}
\cdot & \cdot & \cdot & \cdot \\
\cdot & \cdot & \cdot & \cdot \\
\cdot & \cdot & \cdot & \cdot
\end{matrix}
$$

A variety of strategies that help your students succeed on the test are available. You know your students, and you know best how to equip them for success.

The Brain Dump

Another strategy is to teach your students to *brain dump* when they first open the test booklet. What does a brain dump look like? Depending on the subject area and grade level, it's any information that the students can use to help improve their performance. It could be a number line, a conversion chart, a song, a mnemonic device, or a list of definitions.

In math, a brain dump might tell students the steps to a division problem, the order of operations, or the definitions of mean, median, and mode. In language arts it might state the difference between narrative and expository or give a list of transitional words. When I taught, I would tell my students they could brain dump before starting any test. I noticed that most of them progressed to the point that they didn't need the brain dump because they had learned the information.

You might have a standard brain dump for the entire class. Perhaps you would have a class contest to see who can brain dump the fastest or make it a team effort. Possibly you would customize the brain dump for each student, concentrating on the information the student struggles with. It's a tool, a way for students to dump out what they know before starting the test.

During a recent Super Bowl, Peyton Manning was seen on the field looking at a sheet of plays that he had written before the game. Why does a professional athlete making millions of dollars need a sheet to remember maybe 40 or 50 plays? Because in high-pressure situations, we all have the possibility to blank out and forget some very basic knowledge. Your students are no exception. In fact, departments of education know how important reviewing prior knowledge is, because in eighth grade they give students students a brain dump for the test—it's called a formula sheet.

Some ideas of what students might brain dump come from departments of education lists of items that cannot be displayed in the room during the test. Vocabulary and definitions, examples of problems, hints and tips, graphic organizers, and foundational knowledge are all pieces of information that must remain hidden during the test.

You must cover them up, but the students can brain dump them after starting the test. They can write the items on their own paper. Why should they not put down information if it's going to help them? Empower your students to use the things within the rules that will help them.

The key is to practice during the year. At some point during any day you can say, "OK, guys, brain dump." They would then get out a piece of paper and begin writing. The students will quickly grow accustomed to using brain dumps by practicing on tests that you give them. During those formative assessments you learn the pieces of information that students are struggling with, the precise tools they need to be successful, and the methods you can use to empower them to perform well.

A question always comes up about the time it takes for students to brain dump. Doesn't it take time away from the test? Yes, but remember we've already established the fact that very few students actually run out of time. Our job is to give them a tool they can quickly use to help themselves. Practice learning the brain dump during the year, and it won't take them long.

This might not be an effective strategy for the student who takes an inordinate amount of time to brain dump. You are the expert, and you know your students. You know best how to prepare each one of them for success.

Practice Like You Play

A theme throughout this book has been practice like you play when it comes to testing. Your students should become so accustomed to being assessed in the style that they will see on the standardized test that nothing will take them by surprise.

For example, why would you let the test be the first time the students see the formula sheet? In fact, if students have trouble with the formula sheet, teach them to brain dump the information on the sheet before the test.

Teacher Story

One teacher told me that the metric conversions on the formula sheet her state issued for the test were so confusing that she has her students mark the conversions out when they get the test and rewrite them the way they practiced during the year.

Remember that in language arts most questions on standardized tests are on the spot items. The students have never read the text before, but they have it available to them while they are answering the questions. In actual classroom settings, many times teachers expect students to read text and then answer questions using recall. Demonstrating reading comprehension from memory is a valid learning objective, but it's not authentic practice for the standardized test, since recall questions do not appear on it. To be genuine practice for the test, give your students an appropriate number of on the spot questions.

I touch the future. I teach.
– Christa McAuliffe

Testing Tip

Many states allow teachers to pronounce one word during the math and science tests for students who ask. Find out your state's rules governing the practice. If your state allows you to read one word, do your students know that? As a teacher, you can empower them by practicing ahead of time. Let them know exactly what you can and cannot do for them during the test.

Without the knowledge of what help is available to them, students finding marking "c" and moving on is easier. On every test all year long, tell them, "Be sure to ask me if you don't know a word."

Do We Want Them to Change Answers?

Should we encourage students to change their answers, or do we want them to go with their gut? If we want them to go with their first instinct, then why do we tell them to double check their work? Telling students to check their work usually means doing it again. They have a dilemma if they do the problem again and get a different answer. Which answer is correct?

My experience indicates that some students should change their answer, and some should not. We again need to help students take control of their test-taking strategies.

Perhaps you can give your class a test during the formative portion of your assessments. Collect the test but don't grade it. Then come in the next day and tell them, "Guys, I'm really disappointed. A lot of you thought you were right, but you had the wrong answer."

After planting that seed of doubt, give them colored pencils so you can tell which was the first answer. Have them retake the previous test, with the assurance that you will still count it right if they change an answer that was originally correct.

Now look at the results. You can find the student who changed eight answers and seven of them needed changing. You will also find the one who changed eight answers, but seven of them were right the first time. Have discussions about the results of changing answers with the entire class and individual students. Help them determine the best course of action to take when it comes to changing answers. Your students can take control of their own test-taking strategies.

The SMART 7 and PLORE Strategies

Let's discuss some reading strategies that we can use to help low readers be more successful on the test. We typically deliver instruction to struggling readers on a level at or near their reading level and hope they make gains during the year. Then along comes the grade-level high-stakes test. It can be demoralizing to a student who is marginally successful in the first place. Many times the student may think, "I might not be able to get the questions right, but I can sure get done quickly and look smart."

We typically do such a poor job of reporting test results that the method seems logical to those students. We might give them a piece of paper at the beginning of next year that reports their scores, but is it really that important to them? Students quickly understand that they might as well seem smart, act like they don't care, or whatever other response they choose to have. They merely give up and play Guitar Hero™ with the answers.

A solution to the problem lies in inner motivation to do well—an issue that we will address fully in Chapters 9 and 10. But in addition to motivation, let's give students tools that build their confidence and enable them to know they can get at least some of the questions correct.

Test scorers tell me they see students using several strategies as they grade the reading comprehension portion of tests. They tell me that which strategy the students use doesn't seem to matter.

What is obvious to scorers is that students who have a strategy to use when answering reading questions practically *always* score higher than those who have no strategy at all.

I want to highlight two common strategies that you might want to try. Am I asserting that these are the best strategies? Of course not. You may already be using a method that works for you and your students. The important point to note is to make sure your students have a strategy. Strategies work well for all students, but they seem to be especially helpful for those who are struggling with reading comprehension.

The SMART 7

The SMART 7

1. Read and box in the title/trace and number the paragraphs.
2. Read every paragraph and STOP and THINK.
3. Read every paragraph and IDENTIFY key words.
4. Read and IDENTIFY key words in the question. (Q)
5. Read each answer and put an x, ?, or + by each choice. (A)
6. Prove the answer. Locate the paragraph where each answer is found. (R)
7. Mark or write the answer.

First, we want the students to box in the title because it makes them pause and think about what the passage might be about. Truly, some good information can be found in the title. Second, we ask them to stop and think with their pencil down after reading each paragraph.

All who have meditated on the art of governing mankind have been convinced that the fate of empires depends on the education of youth.
— Aristotle

Teacher Tip

One teacher told me she has her students draw a cartoon when reading. After reading each paragraph, they draw a cartoon or a stick figure. Many students are relatively fluent but have low comprehension. Drawing gives them an opportunity to express themselves. The strategy shouldn't be used on the high-stakes test, but it's a great tool for some struggling readers as they practice for it.

On the third step of the Smart 7 process, we have students underlining key words. How will they know what the key words are? They will know them when they see them because you've practiced identifying them with your students all year.

The fourth step can be a bit controversial. Do we want students to read the question before or after the passage? I've found in my conversations with teachers that students reading on or above grade level benefit most from reading the questions first; they become purposeful readers.

Students reading below grade level either read the passage first and forget what happened, or they read the questions first and become too purposeful as they search for key words to answer the questions. Having them read the passage first in order to get some context might be a good idea.

I say do whatever works for you in your classroom. If your students read the question first and have success, that's fine, but think about the danger of some students becoming word searchers.

The PLORE Strategy

The PLORE Strategy

1. **P**review and **P**redict from the title what the story might be about.
2. **L**ocate all the vocabulary words in the passage (context clues).
3. **O**rganize the information by writing short notes about each paragraph as you read.
4. **R**ead and **R**eread the passage to find the answers to the questions.
5. **E**liminate all the answers you know are wrong, and **E**valuate by looking back in the story and proving your answers to yourself.

You can adapt both strategies easily to your teaching style and grade level. A quick Internet search reveals several excellent websites that expand on both the SMART 7 and PLORE strategies.

You have to think anyway, so why not think big?
– Donald Trump

Writing Prompts

Some state tests have a major performance event that requires students to generate writing by responding to a prompt. Scorers grade the writing prompt holistically. They first read the student work to give it a base score and then examine the rubric to see if it meets most of the requirements.

The graders then assign a score in a range of – to +. For example, a paper might be scored as a 3-, 3, or 3+. When helping students see the difference between scoring levels, comparing levels that are not adjoining is useful. In other words, compare a 4 to a 2 or a 3 to a 1.

When helping students who are struggling with writing, working on the process instead of the curriculum is most beneficial. Key words are *increase* and *improve.*

I have found that three types of students generally struggle with writing prompts:

1. Students who can legitimately write no more than three or four lines; it's all they can do. Their problem is they need to increase the volume of their writing.
2. Students who can fill the page, but their writing is just a lot of nonsense. Their problem isn't volume; they need to improve their writing.
3. Students who are the B+ performers; they fill the page with volume, and it's fairly good writing. They need a little bit of improvement to put them over the top.

The Quantity Problem

I certainly don't want to delve deeply into teaching writing processes in this book. A wide variety of books and other resources from people who know more about the subject than I do are available. *Step Up to Writing* and the *Five-Step Writing Process* are two popular programs. Computer-aided writing instruction software has recently evolved to provide some valuable resources. A quick Internet search yields a plethora of resources for teaching the writing process.

The Quality Problem

A wide variety of strategies to help students improve the quality of their writing are available. Below are just a few.

Strategies to Improve Writing Quality

- To help students find interesting words, have them skip a line between each line of their writing. Then they can go back and cross out bland words, writing a more interesting word above it.
- To help students use different sentence patterns, have them brain dump simple words such as *but* and *because.*
- Another strategy to help them use different sentence patterns is a contest to see who can have the greatest difference in word count between the shortest and longest sentences in their writing.

- To help students write in logical order, brain dump seven transitional words and check them off as they use them. Words such as *first, next,* and *then* help them organize their thoughts. They can even practice writing the transitional words alongside paragraphs in the margin of their papers.
- Having students critique their own or peers' papers can be useful to help improve the quality of their writing.

My parents told me, "Finish your dinner. People in China and India are starving." I tell my daughters, "Finish your homework. People in China and India are starving for your jobs."
– Thomas L. Friedman

We are born charming, fresh and spontaneous and must be civilized before we are fit to participate in society.
— Judith Martin, aka "Miss Manners"

Chapter 8

RELIEVING TEST ANXIETY

The Four P's

Test Anxiety Is Real

I'm sure I don't have to convince you that test anxiety is a real phenomenon. Almost every hand goes up when I ask teachers in my workshops if any of them know students who score lower than they should because of test anxiety, and nearly two-thirds of the hands go up when I ask if any of them have experienced test anxiety.

Test anxiety is a psychological condition in which a person experiences stress before, during, or after a test to such an extent that this anxiety causes poor performance. Test anxiety is actually a type of performance anxiety, a feeling someone might have in a situation where performance really counts or when the pressure is on to do well.

All anxiety is a reaction to anticipating something stressful. Like other anxiety reactions, test anxiety affects the body and the mind. When a person is under stress, the brain releases the hormone adrenaline, which prepares it for danger.

In 2006 the U.S. Department of Education funded a study with 980 10th grade students, and found that 61% of all students reported being affected by test anxiety. Also, 26% experienced high levels of test anxiety often or most of the time. In addition, the study found a strong negative relationship between test anxiety and test performance. Students with high levels of test anxiety scored, on average, 15 points lower on standardized tests in both mathematics and language arts than students with low test anxiety (Bradley et al., 2007).

As early as 1952, Mandler and Sarason found that test anxiety had a strong negative relationship with test performance and developed the Test Anxiety Questionnaire

(TAQ) to quantify the experience. They correlated symptoms in the physical, emotional, behavioral, and cognitive realms to increased levels of test anxiety.

Some Anxiety Is a Good Thing

We can use some stress to our advantage. Anxiety is our body's warning signal that something important is ahead and allows us the time to prepare for what is about to happen. I believe we want students to have some anxiety as the test approaches. It means they care about the results. A student who doesn't care isn't motivated to approach the test with a sense of responsibility and a desire to succeed.

I personally experience anxiety every day that I make a presentation to a group of teachers because I care about the results. I want the workshop to be excellent, with teachers feeling they received their money's worth and carrying away tools that will directly affect their teaching. I would not get the results I want if I'm laid back, unconcerned, and don't care about the outcome. We all need that edge that comes from adrenaline flowing in our bodies, just as the star athlete needs that sharpness when he or she enters competition.

Your students need that bit of apprehension and anxiety as a motivation for the test, but test anxiety can easily overwhelm some students and reduce their performance. Glossing over the topic by simply telling them they are smart, they will do fine, and they have no need to worry isn't helpful. Instead, we need to give them tools to help reduce that apprehension.

The Four P's

Preparation

We must prepare students effectively for the test, but that they feel prepared is just as important. One of the worst things we can do is tell them they're prepared when they really aren't. They will not feel prepared if they open the test and panic, thinking, "Oh, no! I've never seen this stuff before!"

Preparation can be in the form of content or in recognizing question type. In this book, I've discussed several times the importance of practicing like we play. Students should seldom be surprised by an item on the test because we've practiced those types of items all year long.

We know the standards that the test addresses. Possibly we have put those standards on the bulletin board and checked them off when we covered them, saying, "OK, guys, we're going to be ready for the test. See how we're going through these standards?" Or students might have their own personal checklist and take responsibility for checking the standards off when they demonstrate mastery.

We could give practice tests that look similar to the real test. Students wouldn't even have to take the test. They might go through the test, marking the items that they think they know how to answer correctly. We can compare that to the scoring matrix so they see they really do know the content and can feel more confident as the test day approaches. Prove to your students that they are prepared!

Preparation can also take the form of process. Some students panic when they open the test booklet. What do they do first? They need a plan, and it might differ from student to student. Some might pop a Jolly Rancher™ in their mouths to manage the timer effect, while others do a brain dump. Possibly the entire class knows to preview the test carefully first. All students should know exactly what to do as soon as they open the test booklet.

Placebo (or Peppermint)

I won't state confidently that peppermint raises test scores. Improved teaching and learning raises test scores! I'm not certain that spraying peppermint (or cinnamon or lemon, for that matter) around the room improves student performance. In this particular context, though, we're referring to reducing test anxiety. I can state with certainty that if you convince a child a particular placebo will settle her nerves and calm her for the test, it will have the effect of reducing anxiety. Lower anxiety may very well help the student perform better. A placebo may not directly improve scores, but reduced anxiety certainly will.

Herman's Story

I have a personal story that highlights the power of a placebo. Early in my speaking career, I had a very difficult situation. I was scheduled in a sub-standard venue far from home. I had arrived the night before and had at least set up the room the way I wanted it. No screen was available, so I fashioned one by taping poster board to the wall. When I arrived the next morning, the room had been rearranged. I was under pressure to arrange the room again and pass out materials as teachers arrived. Then nothing happened when I turned my projector on. The bulb had burned out, and I had no spare.

It was awful, and I was totally stressed. I did something I had never done before or since. I went to a couple of ladies sitting in the front row and asked them if they prayed. If so, would they throw one up for me? One said, "I don't normally pray at school, but I will pray for you." I started to put the projector away, but something told me to try it again. When I did, the bulb came on and worked the entire day!

At the end of the day, I apologized to the ladies because I knew the whole ordeal was dreadful for everyone involved, and I thanked the lady for praying for me. She told me that she had a rosary in her pocket, and she went around the rosary, asking, "Lord, please help this man." Then she handed me the rosary and said, "I want you to have this."

For the longest time I carried that rosary with me, especially when I made presentations. I could reach in my pocket and always have a reminder that I was taken care of during one of the worst days in my professional career. It served as a placebo to remind me that I can pull through even when facing the most difficult circumstance.

Fall seven times, stand up eight.
– Japanese Proverb

Physical Activity

Physical activity can also reduce test anxiety. Teachers have shared numerous methods of using movement to help students relieve the stress before a test. Some utilize a brain gym or yoga, while others teach students to have a mind-clearing moment by standing beside their desks before opening the test booklets.

One teacher told me that she has her class "shake it out and take a breath." They stand before opening the test, shake their arms six times, shake their legs six times, shake their booty six times, and then take a deep breath. A PE teacher I know taught all the students in the building a special "testercise" for them to perform before the test.

Teacher Story

A teacher related to me that she had suffered from almost paralyzing test anxiety in college. She would physically throw up after every major test. The worst day was when she took the test to enter the teacher education program. She passed the test, and some friends went out with her to a restaurant to celebrate. Sure enough, while eating, she couldn't get away from the table quickly enough and threw up in public.

A professor who knew her well enough to know about her problem gave her a strategy. He told her that before every test, she was to go outside the classroom, lean against the wall, cross her arms, her legs, her fingers, and close her eyes for two minutes. When I asked her if it worked, she giggled and said, "I've never thrown up like that again."

I then asked if she had ever shared that story with a child in her class. She smiled and said, "I will tomorrow."

Did the physical activity actually reduce her anxiety, or was it merely a placebo effect? It doesn't really matter because the fact remains that the strategy worked for her. Help your students find that special technique that works for them.

The building principal might lead a special test dance over the intercom just before beginning the test. Maybe it's a dance the PE teacher has taught. It could be the chicken dance, the electric slide, or the *YMCA* dance. A soundtrack has been recorded from the recent Olympic games with artists like Rascal Flatts singing *Unstoppable* and 3 Doors Down performing *Shine*. Get a copy of the soundtrack and play it right before the test.

Powerful Praises

Some anxiety arises from negative speak that can come from within the student or from outside sources. It's amazing how easily adults can quench the fire within a child by speaking words that have unintended consequences. A parent who says, "I was never very good at math," or "I never used all that stuff I learned in school" communicates a powerful message to a child.

Teaching children to be aware of their thoughts is one of the most important tools we can use to help them overcome anxiety and become successful in all areas of life. So much information and messages pass through their minds on a daily basis that we hardly know what is going in inside children's heads.

If you have ever attempted to use affirmations as an adult, you have found that studying exactly what your mind is thinking in the first place is necessary. It's often surprising that we can trace the roots of particular negative thoughts back to our own childhood. Wayne Dyer (2001) in his book *What Do You Really Want for Your Children?* states:

> The ways in which a child talks to him/herself reflect his/her self-concept. Children who constantly complain, telling themselves that they cannot do certain things, are in fact creating a self-fulfilling prophecy.

Consider how incredibly empowering teaching children the power of positive thinking can be. Help them learn mantras such as those found at the top of the next page. Children can use positive speak for the rest of their lives.

An ounce of praise can accomplish more that a ton of fault-finding. And if one looks for it, something worthy of praise can be found in every child.
– John Drescher

Pretend that every single person you meet has a sign around his or her neck that says, "Make me feel important."
– Mary Kay Ash

Positive Self-Talk for Children

I can do this. This is easy!

I am a good kid.

I am creative.

I am loved.

I have many talents.

Today, I have confidence.

I am a friendly person.

I respect myself and others.

I feel happy.

Good things happen when I work hard and do my best.

I make wise choices.

I treat myself and others with kindness and patience.

I have control over my own thoughts and emotions.

Cool Idea

Not too long ago I was presenting in a classroom on a community college campus when I noticed the back wall of the room covered with pictures of people and pieces of paper that said, "I'm working hard because . . ."

Some of the inscriptions said, "I'm working hard because my brother believes in me," or "I'm working hard because I have two little kids at home and I need this degree to provide them a better life." It was a motivational wall!

Many of these students were non-traditional, and the teacher in the room had them bring in pictures of people in their lives that were powerful motivators for them.

On another wall were posted phrases such as "I did it!" with a date of graduation. Others were short testimonials regarding the obstacles a student overcame to achieve his or her dream.

After a particularly brutal time in my life, I was questioning myself in front of my family, wondering if I should even be doing what I'm doing. My young son looked up at me and said, "Of course you can do it daddy—you can do anything!" Those words from a child were powerful motivators for me. For a long time after that, I took one of his little Diego dolls with me wherever I went. I would place it by the projector as I made a presentation, just to remind myself that I have someone in my life who thinks I can do anything. Be that someone for your students.

Good teaching comes not from behind the desk
but from behind the heart.
– Elizabeth Andrew

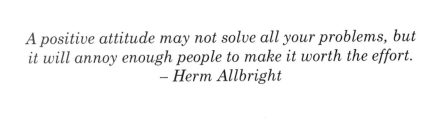

A positive attitude may not solve all your problems, but it will annoy enough people to make it worth the effort.
– Herm Allbright

Chapter 9

STUDENT MOTIVATION

Getting Them To
Do Their Best

Lessons from Kung Fu Panda

Using the Bribe

The Wisdom of Shifu

Kung Fu Panda is a 2008 animated film distributed by Paramount Pictures that has received very favorable review from critics. The story centers around a bumbling panda named Po, who secretly desires to be a kung fu master. After hearing that a much-feared ex-disciple may escape from prison, the head of the temple foretells that Po will be the next Dragon Warrior. The prophesy shocks and surprises Po and greatly annoys the current kung fu warriors.

Master Shifu takes on the task of training the unlikely candidate in the secrets of kung fu. In the process, Po comprehends inner abilities that he never knew existed. Master Shifu develops into a model of patience, understanding, and teaching as Po reveals his skills. The Appendix lists links to various clips, including some from *Kung Fu Panda* that you can download and show as motivation for your students.

We learn at least two lessons from Shifu: the key question that all students must answer and the importance of asking the question at the right location.

The Key Question

After Po has first failed miserably, Master Shifu asks him an odd question, "Do you want to learn kung fu?" Of course, Po wants to learn, doesn't he? That is his goal, his secret dream. He has stayed awake at night thinking about being a kung fu master. He has daydreamed continually about defeating the evil ones who would attack his valley. He wants to be the hero! But he has failed. His dream is gone.

In Chapter 10 I discuss methods to help students re-awaken their dreams after failing over and over but let's focus now on the question, "Do you want to learn?"

Sometimes in education we get so busy doing school to kids that we forget to involve them in the process so they want to learn.

If we don't first ask the key question, we spend our time running after young folks, saying, "Please, please, let me teach you. I want to teach you. I really have something valuable that you need to learn." Many times they just run harder, looking over their shoulders at us as we chase them.

But when we ask them, "Do you want to learn?" and they reply yes, we can suddenly say with Master Shifu, "Then I am your master. Let's begin."

What would your key question be? Do you want to learn to read? Do you want to learn your multiplication tables? Do you want to do well on the test? When we receive an affirmative answer, then our follow-up question can be, "What do you want to do to get there?"

When Po answered yes to the key question, Shifu immediately jumped down off the rock and said, "Let's begin." He recognized the *window of opportunity* had arrived. Borrowing from another animated film, *The Lion King* has a scene with Mufassa sitting in a tree watching Simba. He merely watches, waiting for the right moment, the window of opportunity, to jump down and teach the young lion.

Knowing when the right time has arrived is essential. I'm involved with a community group to help people break their addiction to drugs. Recognizing the time has arrived when the addict is willing to make a change is important for our workers. If the call comes in the middle of the night, with the person on the other end saying, "I can't go on like this. I need help now," the worker can't wait until next week to schedule the addict into the program. The worker must act immediately!

As teachers we need to become masters of identifying the window of opportunity in our students. When we discern them saying, "I want to learn," then we must be ready to immediately jump in and say, "Then let us begin."

But What If He Says No?

I understand that we aren't going to save every child. When I served as a principal, I had a young man in my office whose life was a mess in many ways. I asked him if he wanted to change his life. He looked at me and said, "You know, I'm pretty chilled with where I am right now."

I could have said, "Oh yeah? Well, I can make you change your life," and he would have run from me as fast as he could. He wasn't going to change his life if he didn't want to, but my job was to try to help him see why he needed to change and, I hope, plant some seeds that might come to fruition in the future.

So what if he says no to our key question? What are our choices? First, we need to try to understand why he said no. Has he failed so many times in the past that his dream has died? He most likely has so much negative speak and negative influences that he's convinced he's dumb, stupid, and will never achieve in school. He just can't play school, and choosing to give up is the easiest course to take.

You must realize that your first job as a teacher is to motivate kids to learn. *You* are the master motivator. Hundreds of motivational experts are flying around the country speaking and selling books, but what they are doing pales in comparison to the impact you have every day on young people. Pick up the torch. Become the motivator.

We aren't going to reach every student. I know that. But listen to your kids, look through their eyes, and jump in quickly when a window of opportunity opens.

> *Our chief want is someone who will inspire us to be what we know we can be.*
> – *Ralph Waldo Emerson*

The Key Location

The second point we learn from Master Shifu is the importance of the location when we ask the key question. Why did Shifu take Po to the Pool of Sacred Tears to ask him the question? It was the birthplace of kung fu and it was a place of significance for Po, but I think they went to the Pool because it was a place of solitude. The Pool of Sacred Tears was a place where they could be alone.

What will your struggling student say if you ask him the key question while he is in front of his friends? If you ask him in public if he wants to learn to read, he will respond, "Well, not so much," "maybe not," or "yeah, whatever." It's cool to say no and to act like you don't care to cover up the fact that you've failed in something.

Where is your Pool of Sacred Tears, your place of solitude? It might be at the kidney table in the back of your room, or in the hall, or after school during tutoring. Your place alone with your student might be on the playground. Your place of solitude can be in a number of locations, but a place of solitude is never in front of other people.

A master can tell you what he expects of you. A teacher, though, awakens your own expectations.
-Patricia Neal

The Key Reward

In the same scene, Master Shifu says to Po, "I see that I cannot train you like I did the others." That powerful statement speaks to the importance of differentiation: in our instruction, in our punishment, and in the rewards we give. What motivates one student may not even turn the head of another.

Shifu then says, "I see that to get through to you I must use this . . .," and holds out food. Food is motivational to some students, but I may find that I need to use relationships to get through to Kameron. To reach Troy, I may have to show him that a science fair project is fun, or I may have to instill self-confidence in Alana. It's possible that Steven needs a bribe, just as Po needed food.

Some valuable insight in today's educational world regarding differentiating instruction for students is available, but I encourage you to consider how you might differentiate student needs by finding just the right piece of motivation for each one.

We are quick to place students in tutoring to help raise their skill level, but I fear that too many times students see tutoring as a punishment. Sometimes I wonder if a better investment of time would be to place the student in the drum corps or cross-country team after school to give him a reason to work hard, to feel good about himself, and to raise his total self-confidence which might carry over to the classroom naturally.

The Testing Bribe

Young people like to have a reward for working hard, and I can't say I blame them. I like to have a reward myself for working hard and doing a good job! Many high-stakes tests have no impact on a student's life beyond the internal satisfaction of doing well. Grades aren't attached to the test, the performance level many times doesn't affect the student's promotion to the next grade, and typically students won't even learn about their score until the beginning of the next school year. By that time, even if the student is still in the same school, he has forgotten the test.

So discussing appropriate methods of rewarding students for work on the test is important. What do we offer them? When do we offer it to them? And why do we give the reward?

The greatest dreams are always unrealistic.
– Will Smith

The What

Rewards fall into three categories: Trips/Parties, Privileges, and Things/Awards. The table below lists some ideas I've gathered from across the country. I'm certain the list isn't exhaustive! Feel free to add your own ideas and email me your thoughts.

Reward Ideas

Trips/Parties	Privileges	Things/Awards
Bowling alley	Prime parking space	Nostril pencil sharpener
Movie theater	Text-message privilege	Testing t-shirt
Trip to the park with activities/free time	Listen to iPod	Wizer visor
Amusement Park	Tardies excused	Focus wristband
River	Electronics Day	Ice cream sandwiches
YMCA	Excused from finals	Gas cards
All you can eat buffet	Excused from homework	Money
Mall	Pick food a la carte from cafeteria	Drawings for rewards
Sports venue	Lunch with previous teacher	Two for two (2 items for writing 2 pages)
Local recreation center	Specials with a chosen class	Whipped cream
College athlete visit	Recess with another class	Snow cones
Guitar Hero™	Leave for lunch two minutes early	Free admission to a game
Wii	Preferential locker choice	Free items from concession stand
Luau	Skip day	Free time
Celebration dance	Get into activities free	Computer access
Make a sundae out of the principal		Session effort trophy
Marshmallow shooter (launcher)		Wall of fame
Water balloon fight		Rival school traveling trophy
Dunking booth		Note mailed home
Lazer tag		Olympic medals

The When and the Why

Schools might give rewards at three primary times: immediately before the testing session, immediately after the testing session, or much later when the test results come back to the school. All three times have their advantages, but when we give the reward relates closely to why we are giving the reward. In other words, what is the basis of the reward?

Rewarding after Results Come Back

When you give the test in the spring and the results come back in September, you most likely will be giving a reward based on performance. Many times they include things and awards. Rewarding those who achieve proficiency for you is a great idea, but what about the student who may never achieve proficiency although she works her heart out and shows improvement?

If your reward is based solely on test performance, it might be a good idea to include growth as a measure. The growth can be based on a pre-determined rubric, or it might be growth that the student has determined for herself. We will explore the notion of individual student growth in Chapter 11 as we discuss school, teacher, and student annual yearly progress (AYP).

Never mind what others do; do better than yourself, beat your own record from day to day, and you are a success.
– William J.H. Boetcker

Rewarding Immediately before the Test

A reward given at the first of the school year might be forgotten by April when the next test comes around. The student has the satisfaction of receiving an incentive, but we have to ask ourselves what direct impact that has on overall effort by the end of the year. Delaying the reward until immediately before the testing session might help students sense a relation between effort and performance. Ideal rewards at that time include privileges such as going to specials with a best friend, going to lunch early, or allowing a few tardies.

Rewarding Immediately after the Test

Rewards given immediately after the testing session generally take the form of trips and parties. However, when everyone gets to participate in the party, we've diluted the sense of a reward.

If you don't have a system on which to base the reward, the whoopla is just a reason to celebrate that the test is over, and you're missing an opportunity to motivate kids.

We most likely can't base the after-test party on performance because we don't have those results. In addition, not all children can control the level at which they perform, but all children can control the effort they put forth. I suggest using an Effort Passport Rubric as the basis for a reward given immediately after the test. An example appears on the next page. Again, this is just an example. Feel free to organize your categories as you see fit.

Effort Passport Rubric

	Attendance	Effort	Prepared	Use of Time	Answers All
Reading					
Writing					
Math					

Note: The scoring is be either a scaled score such as $0 - 5$, or an "all or nothing" system of scoring, such as a + or Δ.

I know from experience that using an effort rubric of this sort will drive students to perform better in any setting. How do you measure effort, or preparedness, or use of time, or whether they answered all the questions? You need to have those clearly defined, and the students need to know your scoring scale before the test begins. One idea is to have the students fill out their own passport and have the teacher sign off on it. Maybe before turning the test in, students know they must put their fingers on each question to ensure they have answered all of them.

You can have discussions in your school regarding the categories. For example, attendance is open for debate. Test makers tell us the evidence is clear that students who take the test with their peers score higher than if they take a make-up test. On the other hand, it isn't the kids' fault if they are ill or their parents make a dental appointment on the day of the test.

What about the student who misses one day? Does the student have to go to the principal's office and miss the party? If so, does that punish the child? In actual practice, we are probably punishing the principal's secretary!

My heart says not to include attendance, but my head says I should. Have that discussion in your school. No matter what measurement system your school chooses, it will be meaningless if everyone gets the same reward. You need to develop some guidelines to assign rewards according to the score the student receives on the Effort Passport. Here are some ideas:

Party Ideas and Tips

- If the party is making an ice cream sundae, the number of stamps in the passport might equal the number of scoops or the number of toppings. Coming across the top of the passport, one may represent the ice cream, another the flavor, another the toppings, etc. This year a student may get only vanilla and the sprinkles, but next year he may say, "I want it all. I want the chocolate, the strawberries, the bananas, and the whipped cream."

- If the party is a dance, the kids who get to do the limbo must have all their stamps.

- If the party is a movie, everyone gets to go to the movie, but the popcorn goes to the students with 10 stamps while the popcorn and sodas go to the ones with 15 stamps.

You get the idea. I've seen this work as a motivator over and over. You don't have students missing the entire party because they were absent one day, but you do have rewards based on individual effort. Not every child is going to perform at the highest level, but every child can put forth effort. It's a very powerful concept.

I've picked up tons of motivational ideas from teachers as I travel across the country. Here are a few. Feel free to e-mail me your ideas so I can pass them along to others.

Test Motivational Ideas

- Parents write letters of encouragement for their kids to read. Pass the letters out on the first day of the test as a surprise. What about the child who doesn't have a letter? Have one for him or her from last year's teacher, the PE teacher, or a high school athlete.
- Kids can wear a hat, a bandanna, or a t-shirt on test preparation days. When you wear it, that means you are a thinker!
- Students bring in their own shirt and decorate the front any way they want, but they must fill the back with motivational phrases so the kids sitting behind them see the phrases during testing.
- Have a test prep rally.

- Walk/run ¼ mile on the track before the test.
- Have a motivational wall in the back of the room. The students bring in a picture of someone they love and write a sentence about why they work hard for that person.
- The teacher writes a note and provides candy for each student on test day (I know you are smart! ☺).
- Breakfast Brunch—a morning breakfast for everyone before the test starts. It provides a time for students to talk and eat before testing.
- Motivational graffiti in the halls.
- Positive posters made by students and hung on test day.
- Quote of the day to boost confidence.
- Let the students chew gum during the test.

Meaningful Rewards

Remember that the reward must be meaningful to students. Most third graders wouldn't be greatly excited if you gave them a $20 gift card, but if you tell them they can work in class with their shoes off for a week—now that's a treat! On the other hand, if you tell eighth graders they can work with their shoes off—well, you know the reaction you would receive.

I want to relate a quick, personal story. My daughter Savannah recently turned 12, and my wife Melissa and I walked around Walmart trying to decide what we would buy for her. We did buy what we get every child: a 12-pack of soda that she doesn't have to share with anyone else and a promise that she can close the door to her room and be by herself for one hour every day for a week. With six kids, we have a rule in our house that doors have to remain open at all times, so privacy is in short supply.

We finally gave her $20 and took her to Walmart so she could pick out her own gift. After looking around a bit, she bought a can of whipped cream, four doughnuts, and a new book. She said, "This is exactly what I want for my birthday."

She went home, immediately took her new prizes into her room, and shut the door. When I asked her that evening about her day, she said, "Daddy, this was the best birthday ever!"

Now, if you told me that for my birthday you will give me four apple fritters, a can of whipped cream, a book, and let me go off by myself for an hour—let's just say you wouldn't motivate me very much!

Whatever the bribe, it must be meaningful to kids.

The way I see it, if you want the rainbow,
you gotta put up with the rain.
– Dolly Parton

Chapter 10

R.E.A.C.H. PLUS

Relationships

Examples

Applause

Confidence

Hard Work

The Motivating Teacher

Allow me to restate from the previous chapter the key question that students must answer: Do you want to learn? Too many times we get so caught up in the business of school that we forget just how vital it is to involve students in their own learning. We have schedules to keep, curriculum to cover, interventions to assign, and assessments to administer. The list seems endless and grows each year.

Frustrated teachers tell me, "But these kids don't care." I know that. Really, I do. I get it. I know the reality of working in today's schools. And I'm not advocating that we make our classrooms a circus so that kids get excited about coming to school. But all of us teachers should ask ourselves what percentage of time we spend on motivating students versus the time we spend on teaching them what we think they need to know.

We seldom ask a child if he wants to learn multiplication; we merely begin trying to teach him. If he doesn't want to learn, our job is to help him see why he needs to learn. In the process, if we listen closely, we may hear from him, "I can't because I'm dumb," or "I'm never good at school." Of course, we usually won't hear those words spoken, but we hear them loudly in actions and attitudes. Your job is to give him the motivation and confidence to overcome all the negative speak coming toward him from different directions and lead him into learning.

Increasing research confirms the notion that children's overall adjustment and success at school are closely linked to the motivation they receive from teacher support. Wentzel (1998), among others, found that perceived support from teachers directly influenced students' motivation and therefore influenced their academic success. The study also found that increased teacher support decreased a child's psychological distress both in and out of the normal school setting.

As teachers we should proudly tell everyone who will listen: **I Am a Master Motivator!**

The student must recognize who he is. That the master knows who he is doesn't matter; the student must recognize his potential. The teacher must instill that inner motivation saying to the student, "I have the confidence; follow me. I know the way. I can teach you."

Do you exude that confidence? For many students your classroom is the warmest, safest, most embracing environment they have. Welcome them, smile at them, love them, accept them, and let them know you have the confidence in them to succeed.

Just as the key to learning is many times differentiating between individual needs, the key to motivating students is differentiating between interests. Remember Master Shifu said to Po, "I see the way to get through to you is this . . ." and held out food. We must find the *this* for each of our students. What is the way to get through to each of them? The five primary *this's* for young people are **R**elationships, **E**xample, **A**pplause, **C**onfidence, and **H**ard Work.

What we learn with pleasure we never forget.
– Alfred Mercier

Relationships

In their comprehensive study of urban and suburban public schools, Poplin & Weeres (1992) found that relationships, especially teacher-student relationships are the biggest issue on the minds of everyone associated with schools. Longitudinal studies support the main findings of Poplin & Weeres (Borman & Overman, 2004; Pianta, 1996).

In his book on using relationships as the foundation for learner-centered instruction, Jeff Cornelius-White (2010) states:

> Our . . . premise is that an effective way to reform schools is to foster facilitative, principled, and instructionally flexible relationships, especially between teachers and students . . . (p. xxiii).

Relationships are everything. Establishing a relationship with an entire class can be difficult, although it's probably easier to do with a third-grade class than with an eighth-grade class. We establish relationships for the most part one child at a time in settings outside of the formal classroom. Here is my definition of motivating by relationships:

> A child is motivated by your relationship when he or she will do something simply because you are the one who asked.

I want to relate a story to highlight the impact one teacher had on a young lady. The story is repeated thousands of times daily in classrooms across the nation. Quite possibly you have a story very similar to this one, but this is a story that is especially dear to my heart.

My friend Doug's daughter Janelle had a very difficult year in fifth grade. She was introverted and socially awkward. When asking her whom she played with at recess, she would always reply, "Nobody. I just read."

But something changed in sixth grade for Janelle. Inspired by the election process, she decided to run for student body vice president. Doug chuckled when he told me, because when he found out who Janelle was running against, he said, "Honey, wouldn't you rather be the historian?"

No, Janelle wanted to run for vice president, so Doug fully supported her. They bought poster paper and markers, and she went to her room to make a sign. Doug said it broke his heart when she came out of the room with a sign asking everyone to vote for Janelle with a note on the outside edges that read, "She's not pretty, she doesn't have many friends, she has time for student government."

Doug gently told her she couldn't put up that sign, so he helped her make more signs. The day of the election came, and the principal made a call to Doug, "I just want you to know that Janelle has been in my office all afternoon crying because she didn't win the election."

Pretending he didn't already know the answer, Doug asked Janelle when she came home, "Honey, how was your day? Did you win the election?" She shook her head. "Well, you seem to be taking it pretty well," my friend said.

"Daddy," Janelle said, "I cried and cried when I didn't win. But when I got back to my class, Mr. Ferguson said we still needed a homeroom representative to student government, and he asked me to do it! And I have my first meeting tomorrow!"

Doug said to me, "Now, my girl isn't a student government kind of girl, but that has made all the difference in her life. She's using deodorant, she's taking a bath every day, she's combing her hair, and she talks about school at home. I think she will look back on this as a turning point in her life."

I don't have to tell you that my friend worships the ground Mr. Ferguson walks on. Doug doesn't care if Mr. Ferguson doesn't send many graded papers home because of the difference he has made in his little girl's life. Interestingly enough, when relating this story later to an administrator in that district, he told me that Mr. Ferguson consistently has one of the highest percentage of students scoring proficient or above on the state's standardized test. Is it a coincidence that a teacher who establishes relationships with kids has students scoring the highest on the test?

If Mr. Ferguson asked Janelle to do 100 problems tonight, she would do them. If he said, "Janelle, I need you to get a level 5 on that test," she would do it or die trying. That is motivation inspired by a relationship.

Do you want to know something? Not every child needs that. But for some, that is absolutely what they *must* have. If you say, "I'll give you an iPod," Janelle would probably not be interested. But if you say, "I believe in you," she will work her heart out.

> Not every child needs a reward,
> but every child needs to feel valued.

Example

Two applications come to mind when discussing the notion of example. First, teachers need to be an example in countless ways. Second, students can be examples for each other. Many times an entire class is motivated when you motivate the right student. Students themselves set examples for each other, and you can often influence the culture of your entire class by finding the right *this* for that one key student in your class.

The examples that teachers can set recurs throughout the R.E.A.C.H. process, but I want you to consider one aspect of our example-setting abilities as they especially apply to increasing test scores. Many times we say to students, "It's OK, it's just another test, you will do fine," in the hope that we can reduce their anxiety. But aren't we really trying to reduce our own anxiety? And don't you think your students can see through the words and sense the strain you are feeling?

Teachers all over this nation are feeling pressure to raise test scores. Like it or not, we operate every day in the world of educational accountability. Teachers are afraid that low test scores are a reflection on them and their ability, that poor scores will result in a weak evaluation from an administrator, or worse still, that they will ultimately be fired.

Lately an extreme case or two has appeared in the news about schools who have received NCLB sanctions resulting in teachers being reassigned, but remember those buildings had some acute systemic problems that you most likely aren't seeing in your school.

By the same token, I personally know of some teachers who consistently had low student test scores who were "moved along" in one way or another, but I can assure you that low test scores weren't the only problem those teachers were having in the classroom!

So, I encourage you to relax a bit. You are a great teacher, striving to become better because you care about kids, whether there's a test at the end of the year or not. You now have some ideas and methods to boost performance one student at a time with a systematic plan.

I want to relate a quick story told about Gandhi. Who knows whether the story is true or not, but it gives us something to ponder. The story is that a mother, having traveled a great distance, brought her young daughter to Gandhi. In the audience with the master, the mother asked, "Gandhi, my daughter eats too much sugar. Please tell her to stop eating so much." Gandhi looked at the daughter, then at the mother, and replied, "Bring her back in one month."

One month later the mother returned with her daughter and asked the same favor of Gandhi. He looked at the girl and said, "Oh yes, you should obey your mother and not eat any more sugar." The mother said, "But Gandhi, we've twice traveled a great distance at great expense to see you. Why didn't you tell her that the first time?" To which Gandhi replied, "Because one month ago I was still eating sugar."

To be an effective example, you must first experience that which you desire to teach. The lesson we learn from Gandhi is before we tell students not to be anxious about the test, we must deal with our own anxiety. Relax, teachers. Really. It's going to be all right. You can raise scores one child at a time.

Applause/Confidence

I want to discuss the applause and confidence sections together because although they are two different discussions, they relate closely. Use applause after the student has already achieved the task, or when he has already demonstrated he can do it, and he is ready to do it again. It's the "Yeah, look at what you did!" or the "Come on, I know you can do it!"

Cheerleading doesn't cost us anything beyond maybe a few cool stickers that we can buy in bulk. Applause is easy to give, and it is absolutely essential to motivate some students. We give applause in many ways, not just with stickers. We can also encourage students with verbal praise, with our proximity, our recognition, and our attention.

Confidence, on the other hand, is instilled in a student when he doesn't know that he can do it. Some students need confidence, but before you go down that road, you better be sure that you truly do have confidence in that student. When you tell Kameron, "Come on, I know you can do it, and I'll show you how," you need to know that you really do believe he can do it. Otherwise, when Kameron comes up against something difficult and asks you a question, you might respond, "Well, that was a nice try—you did your best," and lose the opportunity to push him beyond that level.

Second, you need to be ready to work as hard as Kameron when he indicates he is willing to push ahead. He will quit if you aren't willing to get down and dig with him, spending the time and other resources to help him achieve. Remember you applaud over and over, but you only have to instill confidence in a student one time.

A child must learn early to believe that she is somebody worthwhile, and that she can do many praiseworthy things.
– Benjamin Mays

Your Best Is Not All You Can Do

My wife Melissa is a total hottie. She recently began working out by running. She called me one day a few weeks ago to tell me, "Herman, you won't believe this. I just ran a mile without stopping." Although I'm certain I can't run a mile without stopping, I was proud of her achievement and celebrated with her. The interesting point of the story, though, is that she has run a mile every day since. Once she reached that goal which seemed impossible, she had the confidence to run even farther.

What if someone would have convinced her that a half-mile is the best she could do? She most likely would have stopped there and not pushed any further. She would have said, "That's the best I can do." But is the best we can do all we can do? No, because Melissa pushed on and ran three-fourths of a mile and then a full mile.

We must have this type of conversation with that sixth grader who didn't score proficient on last year's test. Is that the best he can do? He may very well believe that, and he quite possibly has heard a teacher tell him that. But is his best all he can do? Most likely not. By establishing a relationship with him, using the KAM = P lens, and giving him the right amount of praise and encouragement, you can motivate him to do even more than the best he can do.

The Best You Can Do Is Not All You Can Do

By this time you realize my fondness for movies that motivate and inspire. They can encourage us, and we can use some of their clips in the classroom to bring life to a motivational lesson. Another favorite of mine is *Facing the Giants*. Brock, one of the players, has already given up before a big game with an opponent that he knows his team can't beat. How many of your kids have given up on the test this year? They've already written it down as a loss in their book because they've done their best in previous years and still come up short.

The coach asks Brock how many yards he can make in the "death crawl," an excruciating practice exercise. Brock thinks he can make 30 yards, and the coach responds that he thinks Brock can make 50 yards. To prove to Brock that he can make 50 yards, the coach takes Brock to the field, blindfolds him, and begins to urge him on. It's a powerful clip about applause, motivation, and instilling confidence.

As you might suspect, Brock gets to the 30-yard line fairly easily, but with the blindfold in place he doesn't realize it. The coach continues to urge him on, and Brock goes past the 50-yard line. The coach gets down on his level and refuses to let Brock quit. He says over and over, "Keep moving, keep going, until you have nothing else left." When Brock finally collapses and the coach removes his blindfold, he realizes that he has "death crawled" the entire length of the football field.

Why did Brock need the blindfold? The blindfold was necessary so that he would not be able to see his surroundings and stop trying because he had reached a goal preset in his mind. Some of your students need a symbolic blindfold so that their best doesn't become all they can do.

> *Nothing builds self-esteem and self-confidence*
> *like accomplishment.*
> *– Thomas Carlyle*

Confidence can sometimes come from applause. Watch the inspiring video clip of Paul Potts from *Britain's Got Talent*, and you will literally witness his confidence grow as the audience first watches spellbound, then begins to applaud, and finally stands in ovation at his performance. Suppose the audience had said (like I've heard some teachers say), "Well, he's supposed to be singing well. That's his job. We don't need to applaud him." Imagine what a spark of motivation and confidence you can instill in a child with one moment of applause.

When does someone lose confidence? Jim Fay, in his outstanding *Love and Logic* (2006) training series, talks about people losing confidence in their children. He outlines the steps a person goes through in losing his or her dream: anger, bargaining, depression, acceptance, and then grief over the loss of the dream. I like to think of the same process when we see disinterested students who have checked out of the learning process. In many ways, they've accepted the thought that they are stupid and they will never be able to learn. Their dreams have died. Part of our job is to resurrect those dreams by instilling a new confidence in those students.

Let me share one more story from my family. My oldest daughter Laney started band in sixth grade on the French horn. She chose the French horn because it was so beautiful. Oh, she loved that horn! But she didn't realize how difficult it is to play the French horn. Quite honestly, neither did her parents! Laney had all these dreams: she would be first chair, she would play in the orchestra, and she would earn a college scholarship.

Band was Laney's favorite class in sixth grade, but by seventh and eighth grades, her interest began to wane. Her dream was dying. She had all this talent, and all these dreams that weren't coming true. Playing the French horn was harder than she thought! She began the grief process, and I never saw her pick up the instrument again at home.

Let me respond to the teacher who says, "I don't believe in motivation, and I don't believe in bribing kids. They should just do well because that's their job." My response is to think about Laney and all the other kids who have lost their dream. When a child's dream has died, and she is at the bottom, she will stop trying. Why should she try? She has failed already, so it's easier not to care. If she doesn't try, at least when she fails, it's because of that rather than because she couldn't learn. And you know what? I understand that, because I've done that myself in my own life.

So what is the point of the applause and the reward? They give children a reason to start trying again. When they have reached the point where they accept the fact that their dream has died, the reward gives them a reason to try. In *Kung Fu Panda*, Po really wants to be a kung fu master, but he finally accepted the fact that he will never be one. But when Shifu shows him the food, he is motivated. Interestingly enough, after he reaches the point of mastery, Po tosses the food back to Shifu. He no longer needs the bribe because what he really wanted all along was to be a kung fu master.

I'm convinced that kids want to succeed. I know we find exceptions, but for the most part our students really want to do well. But the same thing happens to them that happened to Laney and Po: their dream has died, so they go into protection mode. Rise to the challenge and be the Master Shifu in a child's life

Back to Laney's story. She came to me at the end of the semester in ninth grade and asked if she could drop band to take driver's education. I saw that she had lost interest in band, so I agreed for her to get a drop slip from the guidance office and take it to her band teacher. But something happened to change her plans. When Laney took the drop slip to Mr. Sabatasso, her teacher, he refused to sign it! He said, "No, I'm not going to sign your drop slip. You're too good to quit. If you try to quit, I'm going to call your dad." What did Laney hear in that conversation? *You're too good to quit!*

When I asked Laney about it that night, she replied, "Daddy, I'm staying in band because Mr. Sabatasso thinks

I'm too good to quit." I told you she hadn't been practicing the French horn, but two days later when I was on the road, I saw her Facebook post: "Two hours of practice each day may not be enough to get me where I want to be."

Two days after that I saw her post, "I made second chair in the high school band!" Some of her friends replied, "Laney, we didn't even know you were in band," and she responded, "Oh yeah, I'm a band freak and proud of it." Laney's dream had died, but it took only five minutes of a teacher's time to say one thing to resurrect that dream. Just think of the power you have over kids every day of your life.

Hard Work

The question regarding is our best all we can do leads into a conversation regarding the value of hard work. Marzano (2001) writes about the value of schools teaching that hard work pays off. He says that children go home to families that relate hard work to success in four ways:

1. Parents who work hard but aren't getting ahead.
2. Parents who do not work hard and aren't getting ahead.
3. Parents who do not work hard but do get ahead from illegal activity.
4. Parents who work hard and do get ahead.

The first three types of scenarios don't inspire kids because they don't see the connection between hard work and success. We can help students understand that connection by making it a part of our curriculum and integrating themes in things we do every day in schools. For example, choose a hard-work theme when we read books or choose real-life examples that show hard work pays off. The Appendix lists inspirational movie clips that you can download. Don't be afraid to share your own stories of how hard work paid off in your life. Never underestimate the power of your example in your students' lives.

There are no secrets to success. It is the result of preparation, hard work, and learning from failure.
-Colin Powell

An inspiring video clip to show students is the 4 x 100 swimming relay at the 2008 Olympics. Michael Phelps starts the race for the Americans and quickly pulls ahead, but in the third leg, or "split," the French swimmer sets a world record split. The American swimmer, Jason Lezak begins the fourth split a half-second behind the French, and promptly beats the previous record split and wins the gold for the Americans.

A question for students is "When did the Americans win the gold medal?" They received the medal after the exciting race, but they actually *won* the medal many years before when they chose to work hard and practice over and over in a cold and lonely lap pool in the early hours of the morning.

Another inspiring video is by Michael Jordan, arguably the greatest basketball player of all time. He speaks about the number of times he had failed but continued to play. He was cut from his junior high basketball squad and didn't play varsity until his junior year in high school. Some estimate that he shot over 20,000 practice shots, many of them alone in a gym after the rest of the team went home. And we call him a natural athlete!

Remember that many of your students have to learn to play school in order to be successful in your world. Teach them how to play life in order to be successful in the world outside of school. Someone must teach your students how to set goals, measure progress, and work hard to achieve. *You* are the master motivator in their lives.

You can have anything you want, if you want it badly enough. You can be anything you want to be, do anything you set out to accomplish if you hold to that desire with singleness of purpose.
– Abraham Lincoln

I've met a few people in my life who were enthusiastic about hard work. And it was just my luck that all of them happened to be men I was working for at that time.
– Bill Gold

Chapter 11

GETTING OUT OF IMPROVEMENT

AYP

Safe Harbor

Growth Model

Personal AYP

Adequate Yearly Progress (AYP)

As previously noted, accountability objectives established by the No Child Left Behind Act of 2001 (NCLB) creates enormous pressure on districts, schools, and teachers. A working knowledge of the basic tenets of NCLB is vital to educators so they can develop a systematic plan to effectively respond to the challenges outlined by the act.

That being said, we have to recognize the evolving landscape in the world of education. The NCLB Act itself will most likely undergo major changes over the years. The principles outlined here are current guidelines at the time of this publication date but please stay abreast of new expectations as they become available.

A fundamental tenet of the NCLB legislation is that all students in the nation will demonstrate proficiency in mathematics and communication arts by 2014. Individual states may determine the tests that are used to measure performance and establish the proficiency levels, although the federal Department of Education must give its approval. To create more uniformity across the nation, recent rulings require that states correlate proficiency levels to the National Assessment of Educational Progress (NAEP).

States use math and communication arts assessment data to determine if Adequate Yearly Progress (AYP) is being made each year at the state, district, and building levels. All states have a federally approved plan that establishes the percentages of students who must demonstrate proficiency each year in order to be making AYP. Of course, to meet the 100% goal by 2014, the benchmark levels increase each year. You should be able to find your state's benchmark figures on the state website found in the Appendix. Here is an example from one state:

Proficiency Target Percentages to Meet AYP							
	2008	2009	2010	2011	2012	2013	2014
Comm. Arts	51.0	59.2	67.4	75.5	83.7	91.8	100
Math	45.0	54.1	63.3	72.5	81.7	90.8	100

To make AYP, states, districts, and schools must

1. Meet the annual proficiency target in *each* content area for *each* subgroup:
   - Race/Ethnicity (Asian/Pacific Islander, American Indian, Black, Hispanic, White, Other/Non-Response)
   - English Language Learners (ELL)
   - Students with Disabilities
   - Free/Reduced Lunch
2. Meet the participation rate (at least 95% of the students must have a valid test score)
3. Meet the additional indicators:
   - Attendance rate for elementary and middle schools
   - Graduation rate for high schools

The required number of students in a subgroup for inclusion in the AYP calculations is 30 for all groups, except for ELL students and students with disabilities. The required number for those two groups is 50.

Buildings go into school improvement if they fail to make AYP for two consecutive years in the same subject. Districts go into school improvement if the AYP objective is not met for two consecutive years in the same subject at all grade spans in the district. Sanctions for being in school improvement vary according to the length of time the school or district has been in the improvement status.

A state department of education's scoring or ranking may vary widely from those defined by AYP. Especially as the target proficiency percentages raise each year, it isn't uncommon for a district or building to receive accreditation from the state department of education, possibly with some measure of honor or distinction, yet be in school improvement as defined by AYP.

AYP—A Status Model

The reason for the increasing discrepancies between state and federal scorings lies in the fact that until only recently AYP used a *status* model. A status model takes a snapshot of a sub-group, school, or district's proficiency level at one point in time and compares it with an established target.

For example, the target for mathematics in 2010 from our state example on page 183 is 63.3% of your students scoring proficient or above. To be clear, that is not an *average* of 63.3%; 63.3% of *all* your students must score at or above the proficient target. Now suppose your building scored above the target at all grade levels and in all subgroups, except only 62.1% of the fifth graders in the free/reduced lunch category were proficient. Your building goes into school improvement. It's very much a make it or break it type of system.

On the other hand, many states also use an *improvement* model that measures the change between different groups of students using their proficiency status from each year. For example, we could compare this year's free/reduced lunch fifth graders with last year's free/reduced lunch fifth graders. If improvement is made, the district receives credit on the state's scoring rubric.

It's critical that teachers and administrators are aware of the raw score benchmarks that determine proficiency in addition to the AYP targets. Let's suppose that a raw benchmark score of 452 is set for students to be considered proficient on the test. A student who scores 451 isn't proficient, while one who scores 453 is proficient. In fact, there is no difference between the student who scores 147 and the one who scores 451; neither one counts toward making your AYP.

An effective method of making AYP might be to look at those students who are close to the benchmark raw score. Imagine you have 25 students in your fourth grade class in the state whose targets are listed on page 183. You are expected to increase the number of proficient students by approximately 8% each year in communication arts. The 25 students in your class times 8% is two. That means you have to move only two students in your class this year above the raw score benchmark! Remember my mantra from the first chapter:

When we have something difficult to do, we stand close together and lift wherever we stand.

Using the KAM = P lens and techniques discussed in this book, each person can lift in his or her assigned area. We want to see improved performance for every child, but we have limited resources of money, energy, and time.

Most teachers don't have the time to direct attention on every student in the class, so for the purposes of this discussion, let's find those students that will have the largest impact on our AYP.

The same notion can work for what I call the subgroup problem. Many times a school or district can meet the targets as a whole, or at least they have been able to in the past, but that in itself is becoming more difficult as the targets creep upward. Typically more difficulty comes when trying to meet the targets for the nine subgroups.

Suppose you teach in a middle school that serves 450 students in grades five through seven, with a 60% free/reduced lunch rate. That means you have 270 students in the subgroup. To increase the proficiency percentage by 8% is roughly 21 students, or seven per grade level. That might likely be only one student per classroom! I realize the solution isn't as simplistic as it sounds here, but the key to raising performance levels lies in disaggregating the data and using the individual student lens to raise scores one student at a time.

Safe Harbor

The federal Department of Education has implemented some relief mechanisms to help schools make AYP. One that addresses the subgroup problem is *Safe Harbor*. To meet the Safe Harbor provision, districts and schools must decrease the percentage of subgroup students scoring below proficient by 10%.

Going back to our middle school example, suppose that only 40% of our free/reduced lunch kids performed at the proficient level last year. That means that 60% did not score proficient. To meet Safe Harbor provisions, we need to reduce that by 10%. Instead of looking at the huge job of raising the 40% proficient level to the target level this year for the entire subgroup, we can focus on moving up only enough students to meet the Safe Harbor provision.

To move all of the subgroup students up to the target can appear to be a daunting task, but thinking of the task in terms of 10% at a time makes it more possible. Also remember that we are talking about real kids here—young people who desperately need us to help them increase their confidence and their learning.

The Growth Model

Recently the Department of Education began allowing states to use a *Growth Model* to factor into AYP measurements. Growth models generally track the achievement of the same group of students from year to year (e.g. last year's third graders compared with this year's fourth graders).

The growth model doesn't change the target of 100% proficiency by 2014, but it does provide the opportunity for schools and districts to meet AYP by receiving credit for students who demonstrate improvement over time. Individual student growth targets determine if each student is on track to be proficient within four years or by eighth grade. Students who are on track are added to the number of students who are proficient in determining if the AYP proficiency target is met.

Each state is responsible for developing its own growth model that must be approved by the federal Department of Education, but the approach should provide administrators, teachers, and parents with better information about individual student performance and thereby improve instruction. I think the most powerful component of the growth model is the potential to involve students in their own growth by allowing them to set their own goals.

The Significance for Teachers

What about the teacher who, on the first day of school sees 12 Ambers and eight Troys? She is dancing a jig because because those kids are in the bag. Those students are going to do well no matter who is standing in front of the class. Is it fair to say what a great teacher she is?

At the same time, what about the teacher who has five Kamerons, six Melissas, and a couple of Stevens. Is it fair to grade her by the end result?

Because no two classrooms are alike, you as a teacher should establish your own personal AYP. Personal AYP allows you to determine how much growth is sufficient for your classroom.

To effectively measure your personal AYP, you need to know what your students scored last year. Get those data, disaggregate them in every way, and tear them apart to reveal information that you can use to make effective decisions.

Carefully consider how you give those scores to students and parents. Some schools pass them out to the children who put them in their bookbags, where they disappear forever. Some parents may not even know that their child didn't score proficient. We make such a big deal all year about the test, but then we fail to make a connection with the children and their parents.

Testing Tip

At one school the principal and counselor make a point to talk personally with every parent about their child's score, including those students who consistently perform well. They can thank them for everything they do to support support, and tell them that they need their help again this year.

Maybe you can't call the parents of every student in your class, but you can call the *key four*. Draw that raw score benchmark line and determine the two students just above and the two just below the line. Focus on those four. *Keep two and move two.* Moving two students into the proficient category raises your class AYP by 8 to 10%. If every teacher in the building did that every year, the entire school's AYP would improve enough to move you out of improvement or keep you out.

Personal Student Goals

Fixed random objectives are so uninspiring. Imagine a short, overweight fifth-grade boy trying to perform in the high jump. He may never jump over the bar set at five feet. If that is the target for every fifth-grade boy, he will be a failure all year. Instead, we set the bar at four feet for him and ask him what he is willing to do. We help him start where he is, inching the bar up as he improves.

The same applies to academics. We have a fixed random target, a benchmark, that some smart guy at the state department has established for all fifth graders. It's not very motivating for those who can't yet reach the target, and it's really not very motivating for those who can already jump way over the target.

What happens if the short, overweight fifth grader takes a growth spurt in sixth grade? He may suddenly become one of the best high-jumpers in his school. You understand the analogy. Learning can be tied closely to developmental progress. Kids grow and develop at different rates. From the kindergartener who needs another year to develop to the eighth grader who needs to mature one more year before taking algebra, children are unique learners.

Empowering children to share in their own learning by setting personal achievement goals allows them to have a vision of what is happening at school. Now school is no longer something that is happening to them, it becomes something they take part in. Learning goals can certainly extend beyond the high-stakes test. Provide students with data folders where they can keep track of their progress in all subject areas. Let them chart their improvement as they move toward the goals they have set for themselves.

Give me a stock clerk with a goal and I'll give you a man who will make history. Give me a man with no goals and I'll give you a stock clerk.
– J.C. Penney

Personal AYP

Let me summarize some of the key ingredients to improve both teacher and student AYPs.

1. **Key 4.** Focus on the two students in your class who barely scored proficient last year and on the two who barely missed scoring proficient. These four are the bubble students who can influence your AYP and form the basis of your improvement efforts.

2. **AYP Conferences.** Have student/teacher conferences to show students how they performed on last year's test. This conference allows students to set personal goals for how they want to perform on this year's test. Get students involved in their own performance by asking them directly: What do you want to achieve this year and what are you willing to do to reach that goal?

3. **Parent Conferences.** Administrators and teachers contact parents to let them know how their children performed on last year's test. Be sure to thank them for their help during the previous year and show them the goals their children have set this year.

4. **Tutoring.** Evaluate a student's performance using the KAM = P process and then focus on the area having the most potential impact on the student's scores. Usually, tutoring that will most affect AYP

will center on strategies and processes instead of curriculum. Tutoring is most effective when it is incorporated into the regular school day. Sustaining an after-school tutoring program by invitation is difficult, and required tutoring many times can be defeating to student motivation.

One of the virtues of being very young is that you don't let the facts get in the way of your imagination.
– Sam Levinson

Chapter 12

THE WONDERFUL WORLD OF TEACHING

A word as to the education of the heart. We don't believe that this can be imparted through books; it can only be imparted through the loving touch of a teacher.

– Cesar Chavez

Valuable Teachers

I'm sure that you have noticed one theme throughout this book: I strongly believe that teachers are consummate professionals who care about kids and have their best interests at heart. Despite external pressures, teachers ultimately know more than anyone what is best for young people in a school setting.

You entered the education field because you wanted to make a difference in the lives of your children, and I couldn't finish this book without a few words to encourage you on your path. You are fortunate to work in a profession where you have the power to make the world a better place.

My editor friend Dr. Mike Prater shared an epiphany moment that he had early in his teaching career. He taught ninth grade physical science in a school that had a high transition rate. Students were constantly transferring in and out, so it was no surprise when a girl came up to his desk after class one day with a drop slip to sign.

He said she was a small, shy girl who sat in the back of the room. Taking little thought, he mechanically signed the paperwork and mumbled a good luck wish to her. She turned to leave but stopped at the door and ran back to him. Biting her lower lip, with tears in her eyes, she hugged his neck as a little girl would hug her daddy and said, "Mr. Prater, thank you so much for all you've done for me."

Mike said, "Herman, I'm not sure if I had ever spoken one word to that girl personally. I barely knew her name. But evidently something I had done made an impact on her, and I began to comprehend just how important we teachers are in kids' lives. We are probably more important than we realize. Since then, her face has haunted me, and I made a commitment that I would never treat another student like that. I have made an effort every day of my career to look students in the eye and greet them when they come into my room. I want to be involved in their lives and let them know that at least one adult cares about them. I want to earn the respect and gratitude that little freshman girl had for me."

Nothing can replace that special relationship that a gifted teacher like you can develop with your students. Our popular culture celebrates athletes and entertainers, but few teachers are recognized in the same way.

That's all right, because *you* know what you do every day. And your students know what you do, although they many times never express it in a manner that is easily understood.

I'm always delighted when former students cross my path and tell me how they enjoyed being in my class. Sometimes I'm even told I was their favorite teacher! Most all of us who have been teaching more than a few years can relate to that experience. We all touch lives, but some relationships with our students can be more special than others. That may be because we were the right adult at the right time in the life of that child, or maybe our personality or methodology reached the child in a unique way.

Something stands out in my mind as I think about those encounters with former students. Very few of them tell me how much they learned in my class! They tell me how I made learning fun, how I made them feel special, or maybe how I helped them through a difficult time in their lives. But they usually don't detail to me how much knowledge they gained from me. Now, I realize they learned something in my classes, but from their perspective, it was all about the relationship I had with them and the methods I used in my teaching.

Stop right now and think about your favorite teacher.

Who came to your mind? Why? Was it because you remember all the wonderful things you learned in his or her class? Or was it because he or she made learning meaningful and relevant to you? Possibly, it was because the teacher touched your soul and encouraged you to set goals and begin to dream of things you never before thought possible. Very likely that teacher you are thinking about is one of the main reasons you are a teacher today.

Which is more important, test scores or kids? You know the answer. But I'm sure by now you understand that I believe one of the secrets to improved student performance is establishing meaningful and appropriate relationships with your students. I encourage you to make a new commitment to be that teacher in a child's life in the way your favorite teacher was to you.

One looks back with appreciation to the brilliant teachers, but with gratitude to those who touched our human feelings. The curriculum is so much necessary material, but warmth is the vital element for the growing plant and for the soul of the child.
– Carl Jung

On the first day of school many of you will have an Amanda who comes to class wearing a pretty, new dress. Her shiny hair will be combed and put up with ribbons. She will have a new backpack for school filled with supplies. She is bright, smiling, and ready to please. Her mom and dad are proud of her and tell her what wonderful things she is going to accomplish.

But you may also have Kameron, wearing faded jeans and a worn tee shirt. His mother was able to find new shoes that fit him at the Resource Center, the first new item to wear that he has had in nearly a year. He doesn't have school supplies, so you have to find some for him. When his father is around, he tells Kameron how stupid he is and how he will never amount to anything special.

You can meet the challenges you face in your classroom because you are a teacher; you know how to reach the Amandas, the Kamerons, and all the students in between. You are a special person in their lives, and you can reach deep inside them and find something they didn't know existed. You show faith in their abilities and in their potential, even when they sometimes do not be-lieve in themselves.

Your influence is engraved in them forever, because

you are a teacher!

References

Ainsworth, L., & Viegut, D. (2006). *Common formative assessments.* Thousand Oaks, CA: Corwin Press.

Borman, G .D., & Overman, L .T. (2004). Academic resilience in mathematics among poor and minority students. *Elementary School Journal, 104*(3), 177-195.

Bradley, T., McCraty, R., Atkinson, M., Arguelles, L., Rees, R., and Tomasino, D. (2007). TestEdge national demonstration study. *HeartMath Research Center, Institute of HeartMath.* Boulder Creek, CO.

Bromley, K., Irwin-DeVitis, L., & Modlo, M. (1995). *Graphic organizers.* Scholastic Professional Books: New York.

Cornelius-White, J .H. D., & Harbaugh, A. P. (2010). *Learner-centered instruction: Building relationships for student success.* Thousand Oaks, CA: SAGE.

Dyer, W. W. (2001). *What do you really want for your children?* Harper Paperbacks.

Fay, J., and Cline, F. (2006). *Parenting with love and logic, expanded ed.* NavPress Publishing.

Hanushek, E. A., and Raymond, M. F. (2005). Does school accountability lead to increased student performance? *Journal of Policy Analysis and Management*, 24(2), 297-327.

Jacobs, H.H. (2004). *Getting results with curriculum mapping.* Alexandria, VA: ASCD.

Kane, T.J., and Staiger, D.O. (2002). The promise and pitfalls of using imprecise school accountability measures. *Journal of Economic Perspectives, 16*(4), 91-114.

Linn, R. L., Baker, E .L., Bettebenner, D. W., (2002). Accountability systems: Implications of requirements of the No Child Left Behind Act of 2001. *Educational Researcher, 31*(6), 3-16.

Mandler, G., & Sarason, S. B. (1952). A study of anxiety and learning. *Journal of Abnormal and Social Psychology, 47,* 166-173.

Marzano, R. (2006). *Classroom assessments and grading that work.* Alexandria, VA: ASCD.

Marzano, R., Pickering, D., & Pollack, J. E. (2001). *Classroom instruction that works: Research based strategies for increasing student achievement.* Alexandria, VA: ASCD.

Pianta, R.C. (1996). *High-risk children in schools: Constructing sustainable relationships.* New York: Routledge.

Poplin, M., & Weeres, J. (1992). *Voices from the inside: A report on schooling from inside the classroom. Part one: Naming the problem.* Claremont, CA: The Institute for Education in Transformation at the Claremont Graduate School.

Popham, W.J. (2008). *Transformative assessment.* Alexandria, VA: ASCD.

Raphael, T. (1986). Teaching question answer relationships, revisited. *The Reading Teacher,* 39(6), 516-522.

Reeves, D. (2007). *Ahead of the curve: The power of assessment to transform teaching and learning.* Solution Tree.

Wentzel, K. (1998). Social relations and motivation in middle school: The role of parents, teachers, and peers. *Journal of Educational Psychology,* 90(2), 202-209.

Wiggins, G., and McTighe, J. (2005), *Understanding by design, Expanded 2nd Edition.* Alexandria, VA: ASCD.

Index

APPENDIX

Links to Departments of Education

Video Download References

DOK Chart

Links to State Departments of Education

Alabama
www.alsde.edu: Click on "Sections" on the left menu bar, then "Assessment and Accountability."

Alaska
www.eed.state.ak.us: Click on "Assessments" on the bottom of the page beneath "Department Links."

Arizona
www.ade.state.az.us: Click on "Standards and Assessment" on the left.

Arkansas
www.arkansased.org: Click on "Testing" at the top right of the page.

California
www.cde.ca.gov: Click on "Testing and Accountability" at the top.

Colorado
www.cde.co.uc: Click on "SchoolVIEW" at the top of the page.

Connecticut
www.sde.ct.gov: Click on "Students" on the left of the page, then "Student Assessment."

Delaware
www.doe.k12.de.us: Click on "Student Assessment" at the top.

Florida
www.fldoe.org: Click on "Educators" at the top of the page, then on "Assessment" on the left.

Georgia
www.doe.k12.ga.us: Click on "About GaDOE" at the top of the page, then "Standards, Instruction and Assessment." Scroll to the bottom of the page and click on "Assessment Research, Development and Administration."

Hawaii
www.doe.k12.hi.us: Click on "Accountability" on the left of the page.

Idaho
www.sde.idaho.gov: Click on "Assessment" in the middle of the page under "Top Topics."

Illinois
www.isbe.state.il.us: Click on a variety of links under "Learning Standards" on the right of the page.

Indiana
www.doe.in.gov: Click on "Learning Standards" or "Student Testing" on the left of the page under "IDOE Home."

Iowa
www.iowa.gov/educate: Click on "No Child Left Behind" on the left of the page under "PK-12 Education."

Kansas
www.ksde.org: Click on "Assessments/Testing" on the left of the page under "Home."

Kentucky
www.education.ky.gov/KDE: Click on "Administrative Resources" at the top of the page. Then click "Testing & Reporting," then "Kentucky School Testing System," then "Accountability System."

Louisiana
www.doe.state.la.us: Click on "Testing Assistance" on the left.

Maine
www.maine.gov/education: Click on "Comprehensive Assessment System" on the left of the page under "Education Information."

Maryland
www.marylandpublicschools.org/msde: Click on "Testing" at the top.

Massachusetts
www.doe.mass.edu: Click on "Assessment/Accountability" at the top.

Michigan
www.michigan.gov/mde: Click on "Assessment and Accountability" on the left of the page.

Minnesota
www.education.state.mn.us/mde: Click on "Accountability Programs" at the top of the page.

Mississippi
www.mde.k12.ms.us/acad: Click on "Student Assessment" on the left.

Missouri
www.dese.mo.gov: Click on "Curriculum/Assessment" on the left of the page, then click on "Assessment" on the left of the page.

Montana
www.opi.mt.gov: Click on "Curriculum and Assessment" on the top of the page, then click on "Assessment" on the left of the page.

Nebraska
www.nde.state.ne.us: Click on "Standards and Assessment" on the left

Nevada
www.doe.nv.gov: Click on "Assessments, Program Accountability, and Curriculum" in the center of the page under "Instruction, Research, Evaluation Home."

New Hampshire
www.ed.state.nh.us: Click on "Data and Reports" on the left of the page, then "Assessment Tests."

New Jersey
www.state.nj.us: In the "Overview of DOE Sites" pull-down menu at the top right, click on "Assessment."

New Mexico
www.ped.state.nm.us: Click on the "PED A to Z Directory" at the top and then choose "Assessments."

New York
www.nysed.gov: Click on "Testing" under "Quick Links" at the left.

North Carolina
www.ncpublicschool.org: Click on "Testing" at the top of the page.

North Dakota
www.dpi.state.nd.us: Click on "Programs and Services" pull-down menu on the left of the page. Then click on "Testing and Assessment."

Ohio
www.ode.state.oh.us: Click on "Testing" on the top right of the page.

Oklahoma
www.sde.state.ok.us: Click on either "Administrators" or "Teachers" at the top of the page, then click on "Accountability and Assessment."

Oregon
www.ode.state.or.us: Click on "Testing/Accountability" on the left.

Pennsylvania
www.education.state.pa.us: Click on "Data and Statistics" on the left of the page, then click on "Assessment."

Rhode Island
www.ride.ri.gov: Click on "Offices and Programs" on the left of the page, then click on "Assessment and Accountability."

South Carolina
www.ed.sc.gov: Click on "Topics" at the top of the page, then click on "Testing and Assessment."

South Dakota
www.doe.sd.gov: Click on "A-Z Topics" on the left of the page, then click on "Assessment/Testing."

Tennessee
www.state.tn.us: Click on "Educators/Administrators" on the left of the page, then click on "Assessment, Evaluation, and Research."

Texas
www.tea.state.tx.us: Click on "Testing/Accountability" on the left.

Utah
www.schools.utah.gov: Click on "Departments" on the top left of the page, then click on "Assessment."

Vermont

www.education.vermont.gov: Click on "Programs and Services" on the left of the page, then click on "Assessment" on the pull-down menu.

Virginia

www.doe.virginia.gov: Click on "Testing and Standards of Learning" on the left of the page.

Washington

www.k12.wa.us: Click on "Assessment" at the top of the page.

West Virginia

www.wvde.state.wv.us: Click on "Educators" on the left of the page, then click on "TEACH 21."

Wisconsin

www.dpi.wi.gov: Click on "Topics" at the top of the page, then click on "Standards and Assessment."

Wyoming

www.k12.wy.us: Click on "WDE Units" at the top of the page, then click on "Standards and Assessments."

Youtube Video Download Reference

The following website is useful if you wish to download Youtube files: http://youtubedownload.altervista.org

Please be aware of and follow the technology use policy of your school!

Michael Jordan Failure
   http://www.youtube.com/watch?v=45mMioJ5szc

Inspiration Crawl
   http://www.youtube.com/watch?v=T_wyBftd8gk

Paul Potts-Cheering Works
   http://www.youtube.com/watch?v=exyJ2CSfrHo

Olympic 4 x 100 Relay
   http://www.youtube.com/watch?v=Rg9ICvAvBdg&
   feature=related

Stupid Gazelle
   http://www.youtube.com/watch?v=Q8WZQnUWm_E

Finish Strong
   http://www.youtube.com/watch?v=sylm5MHG404

If You've Never Failed
   http://www.youtube.com/watch?v=gZTVX21jPtc

Depth of Knowledge (DOK) Levels

Level One Activities	Level Two Activities	Level Three Activities	Level Four Activities
Recall elements and details of story structure, such as sequence of events, character, plot and setting.	Identify and summarize the major events in a narrative.	Support ideas with details and examples.	Conduct a project that requires specifying a problem, designing and conducting an experiment, analyzing its data, and reporting results/solutions.
Conduct basic mathematical calculations.	Use context cues to identify the meaning of unfamiliar words.	Use voice appropriate to the purpose and audience.	
Label locations on a map.	Solve routine multiple-step problems.	Identify research questions and design investigations for a scientific problem.	Apply mathematical model to illuminate a problem or situation.
Represent in words or diagrams a scientific concept or relationship.	Describe the cause/effect of a particular event.	Develop a scientific model for a complex situation.	Analyze and synthesize information from multiple sources.
Perform routine procedures like measuring length or using punctuation marks correctly.	Identify patterns in events or behavior.	Determine the author's purpose and describe how it affects the interpretation of a reading selection.	Describe and illustrate how common themes are found across texts from different cultures.
Describe the features of a place or people.	Formulate a routine problem given data and conditions.	Apply a concept in other contexts.	Design a mathematical model to inform and solve a practical or abstract situation.
	Organize, represent and interpret data.		

Webb, Norman L. and others. "Web Alignment Tool" 24 July 2005. Wisconsin Center of Educational Research. University of Wisconsin-Madison. 2 Feb. 2006 <http://www.wcer.wisc.edu/WAT/index.aspx>

www.questeducationsystems.com

QUICK ORDER FORM

Order online: www.questeducationsystems.com

Fax orders: Fax this form 573-774-6028

Postal orders: Mail this form to

> Quest Education Systems
> P.O. Box 1004
> Waynesville, MO 65583

Please send me the following copies of
Improving Student Test Scores:

Quantity	Price	Total
	$28.95	
MO residents add 7.725% sales tax		
Shipping		
Total Included		

Shipping- Add $3.00 for 1 book; $1.00 for each additional book

<u>Payment Information</u>

Visa #_____ exp._____

Signature _____

P.O. # _____ Personal Check/Money Order _____

Bill/Ship to:_____

_____

_____

_____

www.questeducationsystems.com

QUICK ORDER FORM

Order online: www.questeducationsystems.com

Fax orders: Fax this form 573-774-6028

Postal orders: Mail this form to

>Quest Education Systems
>P.O. Box 1004
>Waynesville, MO 65583

Please send me the following copies of
Improving Student Test Scores:

Quantity	Price	Total
	$28.95	
MO residents add 7.725% sales tax		
Shipping		
Total Included		

Shipping- Add $3.00 for 1 book; $1.00 for each additional book

<u>Payment Information</u>

Visa #_____ exp._____

Signature _____

P.O. # _____ Personal Check/Money Order _____

Bill/Ship to:_____

_____

_____

_____